Al Capp Remembered

Al Capp Remembered

Elliott Caplin

Bowling Green State University Popular Press
Bowling Green, OH 43403

Library of Congress Catalogue Card No: 93-79503

ISBN: 0-87972-629-6 Clothbound
       0-87972-630-X Paperback

Cover design by Gary Dumm

Dedicated to Ruth...who listened, and listened and still listens.

Contents

Preface

Alfred Gerald Caplin was born in New Haven, Connecticut, on September 28, 1909. He grew up to be Al Capp and died in 1979 at the age of 70. For 43 of those years he entertained, fascinated, delighted, repelled, outraged, lauded, insulted and satirized hundreds of people, places...attitudes and conventions. All of this took place in the panels of his daily and Sunday comic strip, "Li'l Abner."

Relationships between siblings rarely vary. I was Alfred's kid brother until the day he died and I was in my 60s. He was my big brother and remained so throughout our lives. That means he badgered, bullied and patronized me...helped, advised and loved me.

These stories are about happenings in our family as I remember them. So vivid are the images from those early times I cannot believe these events took place so many years ago. But, indeed, they did.

Elliott Caplin

Momma

Tillie Caplin had just died. She was 64 or 65. No one was sure. If she knew herself, she never confided in any of her four children.

In a mother's way, she was always old. I cannot remember when her hair was any color but white. And she was heavy. Not fat, but large. Her forearms were shaped like a lamb's leg, and never without large red and purple stove-burn botches.

And she had died a few minutes ago. My brother Bence came out of her room.

"She's dead," he said.

We stood on the bleak cement terrace at the end of the hospital corridor. I was crying. Not loud sobs, but a low moaning sound like I was having trouble clearing my throat.

My brother Alfred stood next to me. He made no sound either, but he was crying.

Without facing him I said, "She was a wonderful woman."

He said, "She was a pain in the ass."

We both cried a little more. I went home to Brooklyn and Al went to his hotel in Manhattan.

The First Wooden Leg

At first there were the crutches which Alfred loathed. He preferred hopping from bedroom to bathroom or from the living room back to the kitchen. It was getting to school that was the problem. Alfred couldn't hop the six blocks from our house on Stevens Street to the Davenport Avenue grammar school.

Whenever he was at home, Poppa would drive Alfred to school and Uncle Ellie would pick him up. This arrangement was precarious mostly because of Poppa's frequent absences and because Ellie's ownership of his used Maxwell was rancorously disputed by the finance company he had conned into subsidizing the vehicle.

An artificial leg had to be the answer. There were no prosthetic artisans in New Haven. The nearest specialist worked in Hartford. His name was Butcher. A grim, unsmiling man, he measured the ten-year-old Alfred and told my father that the leg would be ready in a month; Poppa handed Mr. Butcher the $25 deposit he required and we drove back to New Haven.

Mr. Butcher delivered the leg to our house. He closed the bedroom door and spent several minutes alone with Alfred instructing him in how to put the leg on and take it off. The rest of the family sat in the living room, waiting.

Alfred appeared at the bedroom door wearing his new leg. He looked frightened. Mr. Butcher was supporting him and whispering into Alfred's ear. Alfred took a step and stumbled. He would have fallen if Mr. Butcher hadn't held his grip on the boy's arm.

Alfred was sweating and swearing softly to himself. I heard him say, "Son of a bitch...son of a bitch...son of a bitch...." Mr. Butcher gently nudged Alfred into another step. Alfred closed his eyes, his mouth set in a straight determined line and his prominent jaw jutted forward. He shook off Mr. Butcher's hand, moved and fell down. Momma screamed. Alfred looked up at her.

"Shut up, Momma," he said.

My brother never mastered the art of walking with a wooden leg. He would sway precariously with every step like a damaged airplane making an emergency landing.

The same person who would spend hours over a drawing refining, erasing, developing cartoon characters with painstaking effort had no patience for disciplining himself in the more traditional values of life. He never drove a nail into a piece of wood, fixed a tire or even inserted a fuse into a fuse box. He drove a car with careless rapture but no visible skill. That he did not perish early in his driving career was undoubtedly due to Momma's precedence with the Almighty. There seems no other logical explanation.

As he grew into his almost six-foot stature, Alfred's distaste for the artificial limb intensified. He used the same device throughout his tenth, eleventh and twelfth years. He grew and the leg didn't. And there was no money to buy a new one. As a matter of fact, Poppa never quite finished paying Mr. Butcher for Alfred's first leg.

When Momma remarked about his walking so awkwardly, Alfred made one of his few comments ever about his crippled state. He looked at his mother and said, "Momma, this (he patted the leg) is made out of wood. Wood won't grow unless it's part of a tree. I'm alive. I'm growing. The leg is too short. I need a new leg."

Momma was numb. She knew, she knew. She had prayed. She said nothing.

During World War II, Alfred was pressed into service visiting hospitals where legless G.I.'s were convalescing. He had undergone a rigorous course in walking given by an expert in the use of wooden legs and managed, painfully, to almost glide instead of sway. The legless veterans were impressed and inspired.

Once the war was over and Alfred ceased his catalytic influence on hospitalized soldiers he resumed the starboard sway when he walked. He said he was vastly more comfortable that way.

Alfred's Private World

There are, in some families, close and intimate relationships between siblings. There were none in mine. Or few that I can recall.

The tensions were always there—Alfred and his awful temper tantrums; the extended silences between Momma and Poppa; the animosity between Alfred and Bence and the harshness of my own treatment of my younger sister.

I try to remember the smiling times and some come to mind. But the aura that surrounds my recall of those years is a melancholy gray haze through which I see Momma unhappy and Alfred hunched over the kitchen table, his hand gripping a stubby pencil.

My eldest brother lived in his own world, and pencil and paper were his wings to another galaxy he created daily on hotel stationery Poppa would bring home from his sales trips.

Throughout most of his adolescent years, before he detonated into active puberty, Alfred invented and populated his own private universe.

These were the days before radio and television, and Alfred's own concept of the world came from his extensive reading and the movies. The movies! Probably never before had there existed a medium that so excitingly dramatized what lay beyond 13 Clover Place, New Haven, Connecticut.

The White Way and Davenport Avenue! the DeWitt on Maple off Congress! And—rarely, it's true—the Bijou or Poli's Palace in the heart of downtown "theatre district." These were the interplanetary vehicles that transported Alfred and the rest of us to wonderful places we couldn't begin to imagine without the images on the screen proving that, yes, there was an existence beyond the ones we led.

It must have been the artless simplicity of the flickering images that affected us the most. There was little subtlety in Tom Mix, Art Accord, Ruth Roland, Pearl White. They were good and most of the others were bad. B-a-d! The Old Testament righteousness of the immaculate cowboys who faced terrible odds with no more expression than a chameleon sunning himself on a back veranda taught us much.

8 Al Capp Remembered

I thank God that I never actually saw Douglas Fairbanks in the flesh; or Elmo Lincoln; or William S. Hart. No man born of woman could possibly attain the physical and moral significance these heroes achieved in movie after movie. Douglas Fairbanks was probably the most mythic of actors; his achievements in *The Mark of Zorro* put to shame the deeds of Launcelot, Roland and Nathan Hale. Fairbanks smiled insouciantly in the face of hazards that would have made Hercules blanch. He leaped, he flew, he dueled with relentless energy and never, never, never broke into a sweat. Could Launcelot, Roland and Nathan Hale make such a claim?

We were poor, but poverty such as we saw in D.W. Griffith's *Broken Blossoms* was a rung below ours. It made us feel favored. And wealth? The richest people we knew were Aunt Rose and Uncle Harry. They had a maid and bought their firstborn real toys from a toy store! But in the The White Way and DeWitt movie houses, we shared the wealth of millionaires, dukes and an occasional king.

Evil acts were punished; good deeds were rewarded. Only Eric Von Stroheim tampered with this verity, and we never queued up for one of his oddities. We knew how to be good and were aware of what badness was. The movies taught us much, perhaps inadvertently.

And the comedians! For ten cents we were admitted to the runic world of Charlie Chaplin, the genie in the oversize pants. To watch this infinitely graceful little man duel with and foil the likes of gigantic Mack Swain or smirk winningly at the beautiful Edna Purviance—this was boundless joyous pleasure.

Or to watch the robot motions of the exultant Larry Semon who fought gallantly the humiliations heaped on him by more favored people. Then there was shy but gallant Harold Lloyd, who battled constantly against a world that wrathfully resented his unquenchable exuberance. And Marie Dressler, Hank Mann, Fatty Arbuckle...and many, many others who for a dime took us to their individual moons for almost an hour of contentment and laughter.

Alfred loved the movies and on his hotel stationery world he drew his own phantoms. His showcase was an imaginary movie palace that showed a feature film, a newsreel, coming attractions and six vaudeville acts.

The feature film starred actors and actresses conceived by Alfred. He drew their faces, usually circled above an action scene from the movie. The men were virile and somewhat self-conscious; the women were beautiful, nubile and jarringly virginal. The titles ran something like this: The Vengeance of Sam McGrew...or...Moon Over Manhattan...or Romance on a Raft.

The vaudeville acts were described in precise detail. The show would open with "a daring acrobatic team"...to be followed by "the hilarious Mary Burke"; the third or star act would be the headliner's spot. It might feature an ebullient but visibly aging Hollywood star "on a sentimental return to the medium he loved best—the stage."

Following the start was a team "epitomizing the grace of the dancing art"; then another comic or comic team leading to the climax of an "extravaganza featuring the talents of 7 gorgeous girls direct from Gotham Club."

Of all the hundreds of these relics of the days of yearning, none remain. Alfred's penciled mementos of his silent years have disappeared and we each grew our separate ways to maturity. The one joy we all shared with equal gusto was the weekly trip to the movies. We would sit in the often rancid atmosphere of the neighborhood Mecca and ride the magic carpet. There was room for each one of us. No pushing. No shoving. But Alfred had his own private carpet: Poppa's purloined hotel stationery.

The only picture in existance of Al Capp with two legs. (He lost the left one at the age of nine. He is about four in this photo.)

The Raid on F.W. Woolworth's

I don't remember where we got the battered red wagon. In a family that bought only necessities, a luxury like that wagon was a remote wish. But it worked. The wheels rolled and the handle extended far enough for me to pull Alfred.

Alfred detested his wooden leg. It hurt and it didn't work as well as a real limb would have worked, so he asked me to pull him in the red wagon. I pulled him wherever he wanted to go. Sometimes it was around the block. Or to the corner store. Or downtown to F.W. Woolworth's Five and Ten store, where the prices were actually five cents and ten cents. There were some more elegant items, of course, for the more affluent shoppers.

Alfred planned the forays on Woolworth's. He drew a floor plan of the huge store, marking exits and counters where lay the products I and my best friend, Abie Shulman, were to raid. Not steal, Alfred cautioned, but raid. Like Robin Hood raided. Like William S. Hart raided. Not steal. Raid. The thought appealed to me and to Abie. We were raiders. Not crooks. Raiders.

Alfred handed me my list. It read: Pocket Knife (for Bence); diamond bracelet (for Momma) pad of paper (for Alfred); a porcelain Kewpie doll (for Madeline). Abie's list was simpler. He was a beginner.

The red wagon was stationed at the Congress Avenue entrance to the store, Alfred seated and observing. Abie went in one door, I into the other. Although this was not my first raid, I was nervous. Alfred calmed me by advising sly stealth and a bland smile.

The pocket knife was easy. I raided it in a jiffy. My confidence soared. The pad of paper took more intricate planning. It was large and flat. But I managed, my smile growing blander by the second.

It was the Kewpie doll that was my undoing. I managed to slip it under my sweater, but it hardly conformed to my skinny body contours. The Kewpie doll's belly stuck out from my belly like a kangaroo's pouch; only I was no kangaroo, and male kangaroos don't have pouches, anyway. I knew that, although I was only seven going on eight.

11

12   Al Capp Remembered

This is no time for sly stealth or a bland smile. I was sweating in an agony of impending disaster. Alfred had drilled me in the art of stately exits. But how was I going to manage stately when I couldn't control the Kewpie doll and the pad of paper? I forgot stately and began to sprint.

A little old lady—she wore white gloves I remember distinctly—pointed at me with one white-gloved finger, and in a voice that could have been heard around the world, screeched: "Thief! That boy is stealing things!" Apparently she was no fan of Robin Hood's or William S. Hart's. Or she would have known this was a raid.

The pad of paper fell from my belt; the Kewpie doll shattered on the floor as I catapulted out the front entrance of F.W. Woolworth's. Out of the corner of my frantic eye, I saw Alfred seated in the red wagon, watching my flight. He sat motionless. By this time, a floorwalker was chasing me. A master plotter of raids like Alfred knew enough not to attract attention to an aide or an abettor. I outran the floorwalker and made for home. Momma thought I looked feverish and made me sit down and drink a glass of warm milk.

About an hour and fifteen minutes later, Alfred arrived. His knuckles were bloody from pushing himself in the wagon. It seems Abie Shulman had vanished, too.

My brother never spoke of the raid. It was our last attack on F.W. Woolworth's.

Uncle Archie's Story

Uncle Aryeh Labe was converted into Archie Lionel in defiance of tradition and the reluctance of Orthodox Jews to accept with any enthusiasm a rabbi named Archie. Maybe today with the avalanche of Scotts, Garys and Sheldons that have all but decimated the Abrahams, Isaacs and Jacobs Jews once named their children, reverent Jews would welcome an Archie, but not in 1922 when Uncle Archie got his first pulpit in Camden, N.J.

My mother's youngest brother, Archie, traveled farther from his father's orthodoxy than any of the other nine brothers and sisters. Even though he became a rabbi he performed his rabbinical duties more in a dedicated personal effort to forestall cultural genocide than because of a deeply rooted belief in his chosen status.

Momma's brothers and sisters, as indeed Momma herself, best exemplified the real reason Jews have persisted in surviving through horrors and tortures that might have wiped out the Ashantis, not to mention the Chinese. They assimilated. Most assimilations involve the conversion of nutrients into protoplasm. Not so with Jews.

Jews transform nutrients into facades which conceal skillfully the truths by which Jews have lived for almost five thousand distracting years.

When you think of it, John Houseman, who sounds like an amalgam of George Washington and Thomas Jefferson with a little of Ralph Waldo Emerson thrown in, was Jewish. Honest. And Benjamin Disraeli, who from all accounts, made Queen Victoria sound like Eliza Doolittle before Prof. Higgins interfered, was born a Jew.

Momma's family was like that. They became more American than Sergeant York. And whenever permitted, performed patriotic rituals with genuine enthusiasm and elan.

When the barriers were lowered, Jews joined the club. Even became its President. They rebelled more fiercely; supported status quo with often dogged irreverence. Sang louder and dressed more eloquently. We were more controversial, more conventional, more persistent, more inspirational, bigger pests, greater poets. They were Jews and each in his heart felt lucky to be here and alive and accepted, no matter how temporary his accreditation to the world of non-Jews.

13

There is a mysterious telepathy between the Jews of today and the people of the Bible. They communicate a nervous series of tics that warn Jews that taking havens for granted, believing that the worst is over once and for all—is *mishigas*. They were created not so much to live as to survive. To prove something. Jews are not sure what.

Uncle Aryeh Labe was all of the above. As a young man his infinite grace of movement made him feel that such a talent would be wasted behind an ancient pulpit backed by the Torah rather than a chorus line of lithe *shiksas*. So he enrolled in a school for teaching professional dancing. Nights, that is. Days, he was a student at the Hebrew Union Seminary.

There was no doubt about it. Archie had a big problem. He proved very good at both activities. As a dancer he exhibited elegance of movement and a gift for facile improvisation. As a rabbinical student, his resonant voice and quick grasp of the most intricate of the mishnah conundrums marked him outstanding. Which life to lead, pondered Uncle Archie.

And Momma pondered right along with her youngest brother. As the eldest, Momma took the place of their mother who died at the age of 48. And Momma was in deep trouble trying to help Archie make up his mind. Dancer or Rabbi?

We were living in Brooklyn when Archie arrived one evening with a tall, thin prematurely balding man and his tiny vivacious girl friend. It was during one of Poppa's entrepreneurial adventures that uprooted us from poverty level living in New Haven to poverty level existence in Williamsburg.

Archie was very proud of his friends. Archie's friends were very hungry and Momma was particularly gracious when it came to satisfying the wishes of her favorite younger brother. The friends attacked Momma's *brustfleish* and *luchshen* soup with a frenzy that suggested they had spent much more time dancing than eating.

After tea and dessert, Archie suggested the young couple do a few turns for Momma and the rest of us. The couple agreed. They were superb. They soared across our crowded living room floor like enchanted impalas; they skirted the dining room's cluttered paraphernalia like slalom skiers on an Olympic downhill run.

When the couple finished, we all applauded. Never, never had we been so close to such divine talent. Momma turned to Archie, his eyes glistening with pride.

"Archie, *kind*, can you dance that way?"

Without hesitation, Archie said to my mother, "Never in a million years, Tillie."

Momma said, "Then Archie, *tierer*, become a Rabbi."

Archie quit dancing school to devote full time to preparing for the rabbinate.

The tall prematurely balding man and his tiny vivacious girl got married and became Arthur and Katherine Murray. They remained dancers.

The Music Makers of Clover Place

The dominance of Jews in the world of instrumental music may have been what impelled Momma. I am reasonably sure she was not aware of King David's responsibility for introducing professional musicians in ancient Hebrew society; it was probably the celebrity of artists like Mischa Elman and Jascha Heifetz that moved Momma toward providing instruments for the children.

Indeed, Momma was possessed with getting a piano for Alfred, a banjo (at his insistence) for Bence, and a violin for me. I had the longest hair, which may have been my sole qualification as a musician.

Naturally, Momma was unable to buy the instruments outright. But her natural aptitude for striking a bargain with even the most reluctant and distrustful of merchants got her what she wanted for her children.

With a genius for organization that deserted her in her kitchen, Momma managed to get the piano, the banjo and the violin delivered the same day. As Alfred, Bence and I looked in awe at what our mother had achieved, Madeline peered out from her bedroom visibly relieved that Momma had not as yet picked out her musical future.

"Do you like your piano, Alfred?" Momma inquired anxiously.

Alfred studied the second-hand upright. He then glanced at Bence's banjo.

"No. I hate it." Mamma blanched.

"But why, Alfred? It's beautiful." Momma ran her hand across the polished surface of the piano.

Alfred remained silent. He pointed to the banjo. "I want that."

"In the pig's ass," Bence responded. Alfred reached out and grabbed the banjo from Bence's hand. They struggled, Momma trying unsuccessfully to intervene. The boys fell to the floor. The banjo held by both was landed on by both. It was shattered.

That left me, my hair, and the violin. After two lessons with Mack Berman, who played in the pit orchestra of the Poli Palace, my career in music was finished.

"Your son," Mack Berman told my mother, "has the least talent of any kid I've ever had the misfortune of trying to teach."

17

Momma sighed and urged Madeline to see if she liked the piano. Miracle of miracles, Madeline liked the piano and took lessons for the next ten years. She achieved no real prominence at the keyboard, but, I think, enjoyed her exclusivity as the only authentic instrumentalist in the family.

Candlesticks

We were sitting quietly in the living room at 124 Brattle Street, Cambridge. Alfred had just been buried in a tiny cemetery in Amesbury, where Catherine had been born and brought up.

My brother's death affected me greatly. More so than my mother's or my father's or friends' I had known in my youth. I didn't think an affectionate word or gesture had ever been experienced between us. Given to excesses in almost every other aspect of our lives, we were utterly non-demonstrative with each other. I don't know why. Or perhaps it didn't seem important or imperative that we embrace, clasp, caress to demonstrate that we liked each other. If we did, that is.

But I know that I missed Alfred and always would.

Catherine hesitated as I sat silently, and said, "I wonder if you can help me understand something."

I nodded, I'd try.

"In the last few months...when Alfred was very ill...he would come down here to the living room and sit there." Catherine pointed to the wheelchair Alfred had used the last year of his life.

"Yes?"

Catherine drew a deep breath. "One day...a Friday, Alfred said to me... 'Catherine, do you have any candlesticks in the house? Silver candlesticks?' "

"I said, 'Yes, we have a pair. I think they're downstairs in the storeroom'."

Catherine continued. She was staring at the mantelpiece over the fireplace. "Alfred went on after a while. He said, 'Do you have any plain candles? Not the fancy kind. Just the plain white ones?' "

"In the kitchen. We keep them for emergencies. You know, in case the electricity fails."

I began to feel seismic vibrations; my whole body seemed to stiffen. I had never fainted before. But now I thought I was going to pass out. I knew what my sister-in-law was going to ask me. How could I—my mother's son—not know? She—Tillie Caplin—dead 20 years, had come to the living room at 124 Brattle Street. Christ—excuse me, Momma—she was there!

19

Catherine went on, dreamily. "Alfred said,...'Would you light those candles in the silver candlesticks and put them on the mantelpiece. Tonight, I mean. This is Friday, isn't it, Catherine?' "

"I told him yes, it was Friday night. I lit the candles and put them on that mantelpiece." She pointed.

"And you wanted to know why Alfred asked you to do that?"

"Yes," Catherine replied.

Momma revered the Sabbath. Of all the ritualistic practices preserved by Jews since the exile, the two most important were circumcision and celebrating the Sabbath. Momma could control one, but not the other. At best she could try to impose her reverence on her children, and failing, observe it herself as had her mother, father, and all the other Davidsons.

On Friday nights, at sundown, the Sabbath started. Momma inserted the candles in her treasured silver candlesticks, a major part of her dowry, and with a shawl over her head, would sway and pray as she lit the Sabbath candles.

None of us knew the prayer she spoke softly. Or cared. We wanted dinner. That came after Momma *benched licht*.

But Alfred remembered. As he sat dying in the living room on Brattle Street, he thought of Momma.

Siblings

We were not a family who exposed inner feelings. At least not to each other. Mama's direct line to the Almighty short circuited confidences with her husband and children. Mama went directly to the source and even at that celestial level her problems were rarely solved.

I learned what I could eavesdropping on Alfred's conversations with his friends. If I had to confess under pressure what 14- and 15-year-old men talked about, it would have been sex. Alfred and Don, Alfred and Matt, Alfred and Howard would describe in detail their experiences with Cherie, Ida, or Bonnie. I listened avidly behind the door to the bedroom and made mental notes.

There was no question about their enthusiasm for girls. The world was composed of high school, uncooperative parents and girls who did or didn't put out. There seemed a strange—at least now it seems strange—reluctance of Alfred and his friends to use words freely spoken today. "Screwing" was about as lurid as they got.

And did I ever long for experience with girls. Grown girls with bosoms and lipstick, not my contemporaries who were generally shapeless and mean spirited. But neither Alfred nor Bence ever discussed their amorous escapades with me. Nor with each other, as a matter of fact. Although only two years apart in age, my brothers avoided contact with an intensity that simmered but rarely erupted.

Alfred was a quiet brooder, never burdening any other member of the family with his moods. Bence was vividly active, rarely at rest and forever involved in enterprises with his friends. These brothers rarely communicated. Alfred couldn't bear the sound that Bence made when he sipped soup and to keep peace at dinner time, Mama had to serve Bence his meal in the kitchen while the others ate in the dining room.

Bence was a fine athlete. I was reasonably agile. There was no way of telling what kind of competitor Alfred would have been. No sport seemed to interest him either as participant or spectator. He offered no comments even on the wildly exciting subject of Benny Leonard, Jewish and the lightweight champion of the whole world! We never thought much about how he must have felt when we discussed our activities. He never said.

21

22   Al Capp Remembered

How did he feel about us—his brothers? Or how did he feel about this sister or his parents? Only once do I vividly recall a physical response to a need on our part. It was Bence who brought on the revelation. Contentious and a good fist fighter, Bence was frequently involved in brawls. It was noon and Bence came from the Truman Street School for lunch, as we all did. He was braced in front of the house by the Brunick brothers, both formidable battlers.

Bence might have handled one of the Brunicks, but two were too much for him. They leaped at Bence, flailing away. Bence fought back fiercely, but the odds were too great. As he was going down for the second time, Alfred appeared at the front door of the house. Alfred had an imposing head and broad shoulders. And his voice was deep and threatening.

"Get your goddamn paws off him!" he bellowed.

The Brunick boys stopped pummeling Bence. They looked up at Alfred, who glared contemptuously at them.

They stopped and left. Bence looked at his brother. Alfred turned and limped back into the house.

It was hard to believe that this had actually happened. But it happened. I was watching out the living room window. I never forgot.

The Champ

Uncle Ellie was my father's youngest brother. He was a grown-up child who loved to play games. Finding companions of his own generation with similar tastes was a problem Uncle Ellie solved by ignoring his peers and encouraging his nephews, aged seven, nine and twelve, to play with him.

We—the nephews, loved Uncle Ellie not only as a play friend, but as a superior being who knew everything worth knowing and everybody of any importance in our world. Especially did Uncle Ellie know and enjoy the company of the giants of our day—sports heroes.

To actually witness a sporting event was a dream too remote to comprehend; but what we could do was read about the giants who ran, batted, passed, kicked—and especially those who fought in the prize ring.

This was the age of Jack Dempsey, "The Manassa Mauler"; we worshipped his beetle-browed scowl, his savage destruction of the likes of George Carpentier, Luis Firpo. But even closer to our hearts was Benny Leonard. Benny Leonard, 135 pounds of grace and power. Lightweight champion of the world, undefeated and undefeatable in our book. And beyond this, beyond pugilistic perfection, outweighing his combination of brain and sleek brawn was—his patrimony!

Benny Leonard was Jewish!

We knew of no Jew who sparkled in the baseball firmament; no Jewish football player of any note—at least none played at Yale—and no Jewish track star or basketball player. So when a Jewish fighter reached the pinnacle of his profession, our Jewish hearts burst with pride.

Benny Leonard retired—undefeated. We were sad that no longer would we revel in his ring victories, but understood that when there were no more pugilistic worlds to conquer, a champion went on a vaudeville tour. And there was always the chance that Benny would come to New Haven!

"I knew Benny would do it," Uncle Ellie explained to us. "When he beat Lou Tendler, what else was there? No competition."

"You know Benny Leonard real well, Uncle Ellie?" Alfred asked him.

"We were raised together," Uncle Ellie assured his nephews.

In the fragile hierarchy of neighborhood society, the Caplin boys stood tall because of Uncle Ellie. He was known by our clique and admired for

23

his wide circle of friends. No one questioned the authority of Uncle Ellie's intimacy with the titans of the world of sports. He knew them; they knew him. Fact.

So when the news of Benny Leonard's appearance at the Poli Palace was announced in the New Haven Register, it made the coming of the Messiah seem like a minor event. Especially celebrated by the Caplin boys, nephews of Ellie Caplin, long-time intimate of the great Champ!

But Ellie was away. Frequently he rented a car and traveled throughout the state of Connecticut selling either "Clothing Cut To Your Exact Measurements By Our Own Skilled Tailors," or a glittering collection of "Authentic Reproductions Of The Great Jewels of the World." The return on Ellie's investment in time and gasoline was minimal, but his needs were modest.

"We'll go down to the Poli Palace and tell Benny who we are," Alfred said.

The news spread around Clover Place with stunning speed. Abie Shulman, Nate Kroll, the Brunick boys, Izzy Danowitz all volunteered to accompany us for the divine confrontation with "The greatest fighter pound for pound since Jack Dempsey, the non pareil."

"Sure." Alfred said. "Let 'em come along. Things like this don't happen everyday, do they?" Of course they don't. How often could Columbus discover America? Or Eddie Rickenbacker shoot down 25 or more German planes? Or Charlie Chaplin make the funniest comedy ever with Marie Dressler? This kind of miracle was a once in a lifetime experience.

And when Uncle Ellie returned from his business trip, we would report word for word our confrontation with his close friend, the Immortal Benny.

It had started to rain when Alfred marshaled his troops. "Listen," he directed our group, "only one of us will do the talking. O.K.? That way Benny won't get confused about who's Uncle Ellie's relative, O.K.?"

We all agreed. Alfred was our leader. He would actually talk to The Champ and we would listen—in wonder!

Drenched by the time we arrived at the Poli Palace, Alfred herded us all into the alley leading to the Stage Door of the theatre.

"I looked it up," Alfred announced. "Benny does two shows a day. He should be finished with the second one pretty soon." None of us realized there were seven acts on the board, and that Leonard came on last. It was a quarter past ten when the stage door opened and a small compact man wearing a tan raincoat emerged.

Somehow he seemed smaller than we imagined. We had only seen his photograph in the newspapers, or viewed him once or twice in a newsreel. He seemed a giant to us in these distant revelations; his proportions would have to be gigantic, measureless to fully express the immensity of his athletic accomplishments. Mortal men—the kind we knew at home, in the grocery store, the trolley car, at the amusement concessions at Savin Rock—would shrink into invisibility in the presence of The Champion.

But this was no giant standing there in the stage door of the Poli Palace, holding out his palm to test the intensity of the rain. Actually, we noted, he was shorter and slighter than Uncle Ellie.

"That's him! That's Benny Leonard!" It was an awestruck whisper from Abie Shulman. The rest of us simply stared as the Magi must have gazed at the infant in the manger.

My brother was uncharacteristically silent. His eyes were fixed on the Champ, but he made no move in his direction. He seemed dazed and immobilized in the presence of this apparition in the doorway of the Poli Palace.

Benny Leonard turned back and the stage door closed behind him. I panicked. "Jesus, Alfred—we missed him. Benny's not coming out!"

Alfred continued to stand dumbstruck. I had never seen my brother so inert before, so spellbound by a person or an event.

We waited, hardly daring to breathe. Was this the last we'd see of Benny? Had he disappeared into the vastness of the Palace never to reveal his immortality to the likes of us?

No. He reappeared, unfurling an umbrella. We turned pleadingly to Alfred. He stirred. He moved, heading toward Benny. The Champ looked at Alfred who now slowed his lumbering gait and stared up at the Champ.

"Hi," Benny said as he sidestepped Alfred.

"Benny?" Alfred almost whispered the name.

"Yes, kid?" The Champ had paused and looked down inquiringly at the boy.

"Benny," Alfred repeated. "I'm Alfred Caplin—"

"Oh," the Champ began.

Alfred's words came in a torrent, as though he feared that if he didn't get them out now, he never would. "I'm Uncle Ellie's nephew, Benny. Uncle Ellie's."

Benny Leonard studied the sodden beseeching boy. He looked over to where we stood, transfixed by the history we saw unfolding before our very eyes.

"How is Uncle Ellie?" The Champ put his hand on Alfred's shoulder and smiled.

"He's fine. Wonderful, Benny. Just wonderful, Benny." Simply mouthing the name seemed to fill my brother with infinite joy.

"Well, you tell Uncle Ellie I was asking about him. Send him my best. O.K., kid?"

He was gone. Bent over against the swirling gusts of rain, with the umbrella concealing the entire upper half of his body, The Champion walked out of the alley onto Congress Avenue, and out of our lives forever. But it didn't matter. We had seen him. One of our number had actually talked to him! We were anointed. Especially were the Caplin boys sanctified, because after all, Benny Leonard's good friend...possibly his best friend in the whole world, was our uncle. Nobody else could claim Uncle Ellie but us!

Pilgrims leaving Lourdes must have felt the way we did. Nobody said anything. What is there to say when you've participated in a miracle? Nothing, of course. Words have no place in the exaltation of an epiphany.

The next day, Ellie came over to our flat at 13 Clover Place. Of course, we were glad to see him. We always welcomed him with a special warmth. But today was different. We had something transcendental to say to Uncle Ellie. Something of such earth shattering importance that the words almost stuck in our throats. Uncle Ellie sensed that an event of moment had happened during his absence.

"What's up, kids? You both look like you just got hit in the head with a blunt instrument."

"Uncle Ellie," Alfred began. Ellie was alerted. Alfred rarely called him "uncle."

"Yes, I'm your Uncle Ellie. So?"

"Uncle Ellie," Alfred repeated. "Uncle Ellie, we saw Benny Leonard."

"Oh," Ellie said. "Where'd you get the money to get into the Poli Palace?"

I broke in. "We didn't go in, Uncle Ellie. We didn't have the money to buy tickets."

"Then how did you see Benny Leonard?"

Alfred's smile was beatific. "We saw him when he left the theatre. When he came out of the stage door."

Uncle Ellie tensed slightly. He must have had a premonition.

"You saw him—Benny Leonard—when he came out of the stage door? Is that what you're saying?"

"I'll never forget it as long as I live, Ellie. Him there and us watching. Then..."

"Then Alfred walked up to him—right up close to Benny Leonard—" I had to break in. The spirituality of the encounter with Uncle Ellie's dearest friend needed enshrinement, and I was determined to participate.

Ellie's normally affable expression had tightened to a frown. "You talked to him?"

"You bet I did. I told him who I was," Alfred seemed to grow taller and more authoritative as he spoke.

"You talked to him." Ellie's voice had gone flat. His eyes narrowed. I had never seen him this way before. "And you told him who you were. And who were you, kid?"

Alfred was taken aback. "I told him I was your nephew, of course. I said, 'I'm Alfred Caplin. I'm Uncle Ellie's nephew, Uncle Ellie's nephew!' "

What was happening to our uncle was something unimaginable. His shoulders sagged, and he slumped down on the old sofa as though he had lost the strength and coordination in his legs. He repeated more to himself than to us:

"You told him that you were my nephew, Uncle Ellie's nephew..."

"Exactly that, Ellie. Just like you said it." Alfred, too, was stunned by the change that had come over our amiable uncle. He peeked at me and I blinked back at him. We had become children again in the presence of an adult and we couldn't begin to cope with what was happening before our very eyes. Uncle Ellie had shrunk the way a sponge shrinks when drained of water. His eyes were unfocused; his mouth twitched uncontrollably.

Slowly, and, I thought, with pain, Uncle Ellie straightened his body so he was now sitting in a semi-crouch. "And what did he say?"

"Say?" Alfred was momentarily confused.

"Benny Leonard. What did he way when you told him. You know, told him—" Uncle Ellie was having trouble getting the next words out. "Told him you were my nephew...Uncle Ellie's nephew. What did he answer?"

Whatever had ailed Uncle Ellie was obviously under control now. The color came back into Alfred's cheeks. He glowed with the ecstasy of revelation.

"He said..." Alfred paused for effect. Even at this early age, he had a flair for the dramatic; his timing was truly of a professional quality. "He said—Benny Leonard said—he said... 'How is Uncle Ellie—' "

Ellie was sitting bolt upright, as erect as a pine tree.

"Then he said, 'Well, you tell Uncle Ellie I was asking for him. Send him my best'."

The rainbow that began with Alfred's smile arched toward Uncle Ellie and ended in the misty beam beginning to form on his lips.

"Send him my best..." Uncle Ellie was intoning the words like a psalm. He was, at least in my eyes, enveloped by a radiance such as saints have when ascending to heaven.

"He was asking for me...Benny Leonard said 'send him my best...' " Uncle Ellie repeated the phrase almost under his breath and in the way he spoke them, each word came with its own halo, sanctified by our wonderful Uncle who knew everybody in the world who counted; everybody who amounted to something.

Not that he needed it, mind you, but in our neighborhood and until we moved from 13 Clover Place, New Haven to 923 Kossuth St. in Bridgeport...Uncle Ellie was canonized. And deservedly so!

Books, Books, Books

My father's parents, Bubba and Zayde Caplin, lived in modified affluence at 53 Sylvan Avenue, New Haven, Connecticut. *Bubba* was small and round, blue-eyed, with a nose shaped like a koala bear. She was a kindly disposed woman who never admitted that Alfred, Bence and I were disappointments as scholars and grandchildren.

Zayde, on the other hand, actively regretted our existence. He rarely addressed us, confining his communication with his three grandsons to heavy sighs and skyward (toward Jehovah) glances. His single functioning eye (the right one was a brilliant cobalt blue imitation) widened with fruitless indignation each time he looked in our direction.

But they tolerated us, especially Alfred, the first born of the first born, Otto Philip. Zayde (Samuel) had arrived in the promised land from Riga, Latvia. He bore the absurd name of Cowper, a mystery never convincingly explained by any member of his family. Advised by a fellow Litvak that his dry goods and notions store couldn't possibly prosper with a *goyishe* name like Cowper, Zayde changed it to Caplan for no verifiable reason other than it sounded more Jewish than Cowper.

Samuel Caplan was a small, delicately constructed man with marvelously sculpted features. His nose was fine and flared sensitively in moments of fervor or suffering. We never actually had a full view of his whole head since he was always covered with a hat or *yarmulke*. His only observable weakness was his passion for Chicklets, a peppermint-coated lozenge of chewing gum which he chewed incessantly. Only rarely would he offer a Chicklet to one of his grandsons.

Zayde lived for his apron-making factory, employing a dozen Italian matrons, and for the Orthodox *shul* he founded in an alley off Oak Street, New Haven's main shopping district for the foreign born.

New Haven was (and still is) a schizoid city consisting of parks, serene elm-shaded neighborhoods, slums, nearby beaches, a varied ethnic variety—and Yale University. There is little if any connection between the institution of higher learning and the nitty gritty of city survival. Zayde was part of the ethnic variety in spite of the fact that his eldest son, Poppa, yearned across the vast abyss of social distinctions and overt anti-semitism of the University for the heady distinction of a Yale diploma. He had faced his father with this fanatic urge, assuring him that going to the University was a kind of religious (Orthodox, naturally) experience. As proof, he pointed to the Hebrew letters on Yale's coat of arms to assure his father that Eli Yale was indeed one of the Chosen People. Who else, Poppa reasoned, but a Jewish mother and father, would name a child Eli?

My father entered Yale in 1904.

The University infected our lives as it had my father's, but with one significant variance. Otto Caplin's father could afford to send his son to an expensive Ivy League school. Otto Philip never even came close.

Alfred enjoyed visiting his grandparents not simply on holidays, but whenever he had the chance. He would spend hours fingering, cutting pages, and occasionally reading the beautifully bound sets of books that were ordered by my father and proudly flanked the piano that was never played.

On the scrupulously dusted books shelved, Alfred found the complete works of John Fox, Jr., who wrote such temporary classics as *The Kentuckians, The Shepherd of Kingdom Come, The Trail of the Lonesome Pine*, and many others which Alfred adored—until the age of 13.

On the edge of adolescence, Alfred's taste in books changed radically. He discarded Zayde's conventional collection of popular authors and began to explore Ford Maddox Ford, Bernard Shaw, James Cabell, and the works of "The Great Iconoclast," William Cowper Brann.

Brann's views fascinated Alfred. The journal he edited, *The Iconoclast*, Brann said, was "designed to break foolish idols and shatter false ideals." Brann lead a violent life and was unrelenting in his attacks of what he considered sham and fraud. He died in a pistol fight in Waco, Texas, in 1898.

Dickens, too, touched Alfred. The ruthless honesty of the man, coupled with his sometimes aggravating sentiment, could be found in Dogpatch, U.S.A., home of the Yokums who, like Dickens' creatures, survived poverty and prejudice, often hilariously.

On those rare gala happenings when Alfred found himself with money beyond the few pennies Momma gave each of her children for sweets, he headed for Whitlocks, the premier bookstore of our town. Whitlocks was vast, like Monte Cristo's cave, and like the cave, littered with treasure. Here it was that Alfred discovered the bound editions of *Harper's Monthly*.

Harper's nurtured almost every young author of the day. Founded in

1850, it began its publishing career by excerpting from the works of leading English authors, and also included in its pages the inaugural efforts of Mark Twain, whose name appeared as "Mark Swain," William Dean Howells, Edith Wharton, Walt Whitman, Henry James, Bret Harte. An abbreviated version of *Moby Dick* was run, written by the yet undiscovered Herman Melville.

The great illustrators of the day worked for *Harper's*, including the vividly remembered Howard Pyle. The bound editions of the publications were scuffed and mostly second-hand, but the pages were reverently intact. For a quarter, Alfred could tote home a ten-pound mother lode of literary nuggets. Whitlock's bookstore was long walk from our house, but Alfred covered the three miles up and the three miles back like a joyous bird in flight.

Lured by the overt friendliness of coupon advertisements in magazines and newspapers, Alfred also filled out and mailed forms that offered "absolutely with no obligation" set of works by famous authors.

For a period of several years, sturdily packed volumes of the complete works of Joseph Conrad, Anthony Trollope, William Thackeray and others would arrive at our house. Alfred would devour the books and generously loan copies to his more sophisticated friends. Momma was too busy to explore the mysterious arrival of these expensive books—until formidable letters began to arrive addressed to "Alfred Caplin, Esquire" (my father had changed his name from "Caplan" to "Caplin").

As the flow of letters to "Alfred Caplin, Esquire" became more frequent, Momma opened one. This missive threatened instant police action if the books (The Conrad Series) were not paid for or returned. Momma hastily packed whatever volumes she could find and mailed them, parcel post, back to the irate publisher. Alfred didn't seem to mind very much. He was a reader, not a collector.

Our Father

The relationship between our father and Alfred was that of two contemporaries. Poppa must have recognized Alfred's uniqueness even before the accident set him further apart from his peers.

Alfred never raised his voice to his father. Against Momma and the rest of the world, he was in constant combat. But Poppa was home very rarely. He would arrive usually after we had all gone to bed. In the morning, we would look out our bedroom window and see his car. Poppa had come and that meant for a few days or even a week we would act like we were rich kids with an indulgent parent.

And our father treated his eldest son with great respect. He listened when Alfred chose to talk. He encouraged Alfred to draw and when Alfred expressed his desire to go to Art School, my father was overjoyed.

Together the father and son drove to Philadelphia where Alfred was enrolled in the Philadelphia School of Fine Arts. Poppa paid the matriculation fee and headed west toward his sales area, Ohio.

Three months later, Momma greeted the grim 17-year-old. He had been dismissed from the art school for non-payment of tuition and had hitchhiked home to Bridgeport.

"Your father," Momma spoke in a tragic whisper. "Your father."

"It wasn't his fault," Alfred told her.

He never blamed my father for any of the crises that developed in a family constantly struggling to survive.

Not so, Momma. The erosions of a lifetime of disillusion with Otto Caplin had made her shrewish. When glittering plan after glittering plan of his had failed, Momma would face him angrily in our presence and say... "First, before you set the world on fire with your schemes, bread should be on the table."

We as his children, never lost faith in our father's future although where he went or how he lived when he drove off to sell his industrial oils remained a mystery to all of us. Regularly, Poppa would quit his sales job and open up his own business. Quite often the financing came from one of the few prosperous relatives in his or Momma's family.

The first enterprise that engaged our father was financed with the

$1000 paid to him by the New Haven Trolley Car Company in compensation for the loss of Alfred's leg. Poppa opened a wholesale silk store. It failed.

A few years after the silk store debacle, Poppa launched in succession a boot store, a wholesale toy outlet, another silk stocking emporium, and took numerous flyers in industrial oil supplies. All that remained of these incursions into the world of entrepreneurship were thousands of sheets of expensively embossed letterheads. And debts that were never paid.

Poppa never apologized or explained his failed efforts. Somehow, after each debacle, he managed to cadge enough cash to make a down payment on an automobile and set out yet again for the Midwest to sell his industrial oils. When it took longer than usual for him to send home a commission check, Momma coped with a grim consecration to the health and well-being of her children.

When years later I would talk to Alfred about the curious inability of our well-educated, charming and intelligent father to make a living, Alfred said:

"He was a dreamer. He wanted to be a writer. He did his best and never deserted us. Poppa was O.K."

Overnight in Greenwich Village

When Alfred left home, a kind of peace took over. It was a mood of apprehensive relief, like the end of a pain we'd gotten used to and actually missed once it was gone.

Hitchhiking or bumming was the only recognized form of travel we knew. Going anywhere by paid conveyance was unthinkable. Even if we could afford it. A flexible thumb and endless stamina was all one needed to get from Boston to New York.

So I started out bumming to New York to see Alfred. I was 15 but mature in the ways of highways travel. It was about 1:30 the following morning that I arrived in New York, very hungry but wildly excited by the feverish atmosphere of this city even at that hour.

The subway took me to Christopher Street. I found number 13 and walked up to the second floor where I knew Alfred had a room. None of the doors had name plates, so I knocked on all of them. From the center room I heard a voice that sounded familiar.

The voice called: "Door's open."

It was. I opened it and found myself in bed with Alfred.

The room was tiny and the bed took up every inch of space in that cramped area. Alfred explained to me he hadn't planned it so, but if a girl should happen to knock and enter, she was instantly in bed with him. Even at 15 I realized what an advantage this could be.

Once away from home, Alfred seemed free from the tensions that made living with him so threatening. He was gracious and warm, offering all or any part of what he had to me or any friend who happened by.

It was after two in the morning when he had his artificial leg strapped on and we went searching for food. Although it was I who had survived the past day and a half with no more than a coke and a nickel bag of salted peanuts, it was Alfred who ordered a double dish of pickled pigs' knuckles that seemed to me to have drowned tragically in a sea of yellowish brine. He urged me to have the same, but I demurred. It was too late, I was too tired and pickled pigs' knuckles turned my stomach to the point that food— any food at all—would have made me throw up.

Alfred had managed to get a job with a toy company through a friend

35

whose uncle owned the outfit. It was only a matter of time, he told me, before the uncle found out that Alfred couldn't design boxes or mechanical windup toys.

"But what the hell, I think I can get another week on it and when he cans me I'll find another job."

Alfred lasted that week and almost a month longer. With the money he earned he invested in a derby and a hounds-tooth sport jacket. The jacket lasted until I inherited it a couple of years later. The derby was annihilated by a stiff breeze that blew it into the middle of heavy Fifth Avenue traffic on Easter Sunday.

Finally fired by his friend's vengeful uncle, Alfred returned to Boston. Although his career as a toy designer was an obvious failure, Alfred felt that his future lay in art. Drawing people, that is, not dreaming up mechanical gimmicks.

He reentered art school and waited. Years later he told me he didn't know what he expected to happen, but he was certain something would. What happened was the sudden appearance of a frayed Boston newspaper reporter who was looking for an artist with a sense of humor. Bob H. had interviewed several art school directors in the Boston Area and two of them had actually suggested Alfred Caplin as an artist who preferred drawing funny people to copying Fragonard or Manet.

Bob H. came to our house with several weeks' continuity for a comic strip he called, "The Jobs of Jasper." Jasper was a virtually unemployable young man who caused confusion and panic with every position he managed to cadge. Alfred was excited at the offer and threw himself into the job of drawing six weeks of the strip. At last he was drawing people who were supposed to be as ludicrous as they were human. Just like in real life, Alfred exulted.

I was pressed into service as a model for Jasper. Alfred's one suit was my costume. Although as tall as my older brother, I was almost painfully thin. The one suit was the proper length, but it featured wide padded shoulders that extended beyond my legitimate anatomy like a bomber's wings on a fighter fuselage.

"Jasper" proved unsalable, but it fueled Alfred's dream of drawing funny people for a living. He quit art school a hair's breadth before he was about to be dismissed for non-payment of tuition.

Back to New York went Alfred, and miracle of miracles he got a job at the Associated Press drawing a panel, "Mr. Gilfeather," that had been created by Mike Dorgan, brother of the revered cartoonist Tad Dorgan.

The Camerons

Growing up I never thought of it. I mean the duality of a parent's role. As a mother or father, we become what we imagine the children want us to be. And often we become that in actual fact.

No matter how intimate a child becomes with his parents, there is always present a vast abyss that separates them—the same abyss that distinguishes man from God. I still have photographs of my father at age five. The little boy is staring seriously out from under a flat pancake-type hat that suggests the one enshrined on film by Buster Keaton. He wears an Eton collar, a velvet jacket and vein-constricting trousers that end just below the knee. Here is a child, and although he changed surprisingly little in the years I knew him, I cannot possibly relate this benignly vacant boy to Otto, my father.

And my mother's non-stop devotion to her children must have never had a beginning. Rather, it was always there, it seemed to me, from the hour she first drew breath. God forbid she ever giggle foolishly or make a flirtatious gesture. Even toward my father. God forbid! Momma was our mother, not a female, or a woman or even a human being as non-parents often were. She was solely, uniquely, exclusively our mother.

Alfred, who orbited on his own axis, must have felt this cosmos of parenthood existed in spite of all logic of the contrary. The limitations and excesses of our own lifestyle have little or no carry over to the modus operandi attempted by our children.

He (as we all did) first imposed, then suffered when our authority was breached by the rebellious adolescence of his children. The Capp first home was in a modest neighborhood in Cambridge, Massachusetts. Although they moved twice, the Capp family remained in this city.

Early on, when "Li'l Abner" began to earn more money than Alfred had ever dreamed of, he bought a simple house and tract of land in North Hampton, New Hampshire, for the spring and summer months. It was dedicated to the three children and gave them ample space to romp and play in the lovely countryside. The ancient farmhouse was charmingly inadequate and remained so for many years. But the children adored the farm as did Catherine.

Alfred accepted the place with a grim determination not to show his dismay at the bucolic nature of the retreat. He was almost unrecognizable in their rural gulag. When we visited him there, his face was ashen with self-condemnation that he could not possibly exist for more than a few days at a time in this leafy purgatory.

But he sacrificed himself as our mother had in the interest of the children. Not, mind you, with the almost mindless devotion of Momma, but nevertheless with probably more pain than our mother ever suffered being our parent.

Momma on occasion would visit the farm. In the midst of Catherine's infinitely New England family and friends, Momma became one of them. As did Alfred. It amazed me to hear my mother and brother assume personalities that would have made Nathaniel Hawthorne look and sound like an intruder.

Momma, who in moments of passion or nostalgia, would revert to the tongue of her mother and often lace her conversation with Yiddishisms of unduplicable quality managed to sound authentically Yankee at Alfred's farm.

And Alfred, whose command of colorful obscenities was utter, never swore, raised his voice or behaved less well deported than Oliver Wendell Holmes. He could nod pleasantly and authentically in a talk with Cousin Theodore, a full time farmer and dairyman whose main conversational thrust was the high cost of seed and the low production of his livestock.

It is true, however, that Alfred's eyes would glaze over midway in the dialogue. But Cousin Theodore never seemed to notice. Perhaps it was the Oliver Wendell Holmes in him.

The astonishing adjustment Momma made to Catherine's family and friends started when Alfred, a student at the Designer's Art School in Boston, began asking Momma to double the number of sandwiches she packed for him each school morning.

Momma's sandwiches were hard bialy rolls packed with chopped liver, chopped herring, wurst (Kosher, of course), or sardines seasoned with Momma's special sauce, and egg salad. They were unmistakably Jewish in content and personality, as was the stained brown paper bag that Momma provided for Alfred. Inevitably, a piece of fruit and a thick slice of honey cake completed the lunch bundle.

"You want two sandwiches?" Momma inquired.

"If it's chopped liver, yes. Two."

Momma, who never mastered the art of reticence or thought

concealment, said, "Is it for you or someone else, Alfred?"

Alfred reddened and didn't answer. Momma shrugged and made an extra chopped liver sandwich.

After months of doubling on the sandwich production, Momma demanded an explanation. She was reasonably sure that her son was selling, trading or courting a girl with a giant appetite for chopped liver on bialys. Of course, it was Catherine. Catherine Wingate Cameron, actually, from the tiny Massachusetts town of Amesbury close to the New Hampshire border.

Catherine's features, matchless in their perfection, could be found only on commemorative coins, or drawings by Charles Dana Gibson. The face that might have been immobilized by its impeccable proportions was made joyous by the warmth of Catherine's personality. She seemed quite removed from her beauty; even without her stunning looks and friendly charm, she would have won Alfred's heart. She loved his humor and admired his art.

And she adored Momma's chopped liver on hard bialys.

The courtship was intense, chaotic and shot through with crises brought on by Alfred's constant state of bankruptcy. There was never enough money for a conventional date. Any excess cash Alfred would immediately invest in a package of Camels. There was nothing left over for the crudest of luxuries. And, not surprisingly, Catherine didn't seem to mind.

Catherine goaded the reluctant Alfred into what he considered a hazardous visit to Amesbury to visit her parents. My brother had never been a parent favorite. Mothers and fathers of girls he courted looked at him with an unacceptable mixture of pity, suspicion and contempt.

Colin Cameron, Catherine's father, was a huge man, who, in spite of his bulk, never seemed to intrude on your privacy. His skin was ruddy, topped by a shock of snow white hair. He was once described as resembling a polar bear in August.

Della, tiny as a puppet, smiled with such tender benevolence you felt you were being forgiven (and even blessed) for a sin you hadn't committed. Alfred loved them immediately. And they loved him.

Years later when Colin and Della died, I had the feeling they had quietly packed some suitcases and left on an extended trip without burdening their family and friends with an itinerary. They were that thoughtful and considerate.

Catherine and Al at Seabrook Beach, New Hampshire, 1931.

With Catherine at Seabrook Beach, New Hampshire, 1932.

Catherine and Al Capp.

Al Capp and his first daughter,
Julie in 1934.

The Capps at home in Cambridge, Massachusetts. From left, Julie, Al, Catherine and new addition Cathy. 1936.

While in Hollywood during the 1940 trip, Capp met many Hollywood stars, Lucille Ball among them.

In 1941, Catherine and Al made a personal appearance at the Sadie Hawkins Day race and dance at Rock Island, NY.

Al Capp escorts his sister, Madeline, down the aisle on her wedding day, August 14, 1946.

Al Capp with Dorothy Lamour.

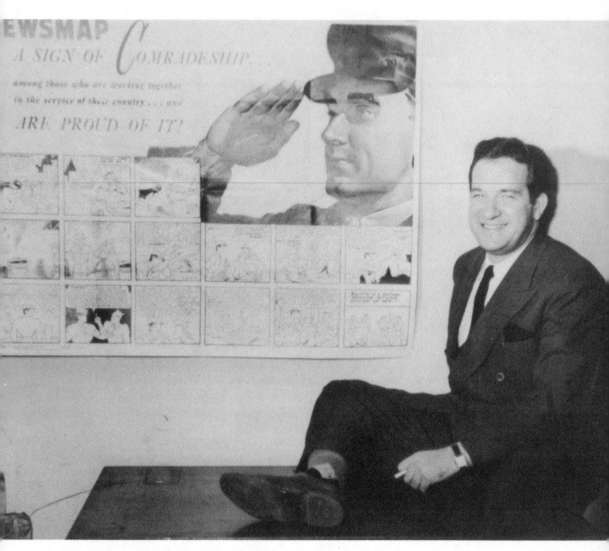

Al Capp poses with his lesson on saluting, 1943.

Al Capp with Ronald Coleman.

Al Capp meets Veronica Lake, inspiration of "Cherry Blossom." The inscription reads: "To Al, creator of my greatest competitor, Cherry Blossom. May good luck always be yours. Sincerely, Veronica Lake." Lake's trademark "peekaboo" hairstyle was a prewar fashion hit.

A pencil sketch of Tillie Caplin done by her son Alfred in the early 1920s. Inset, a photo of Al Capp and his mother, 1945.

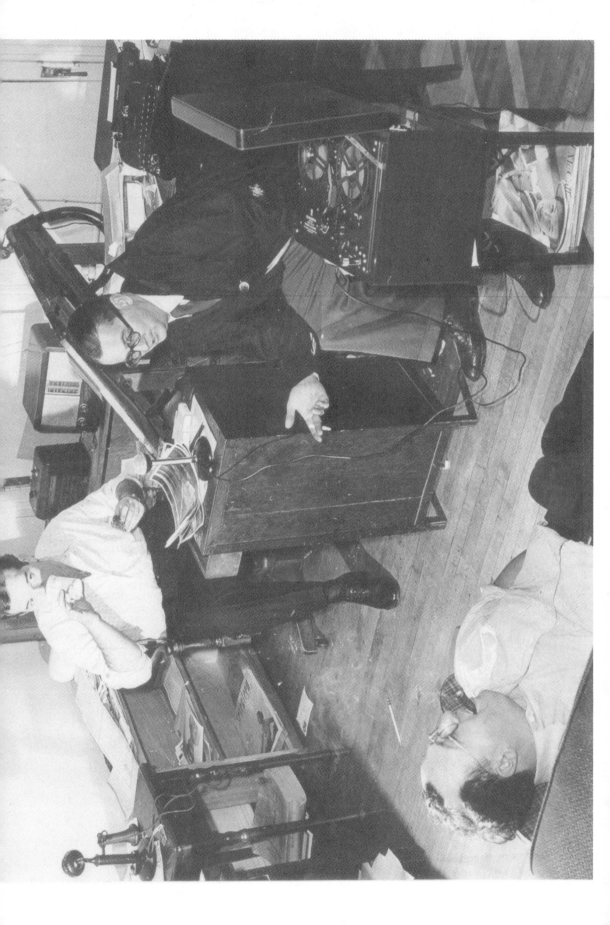

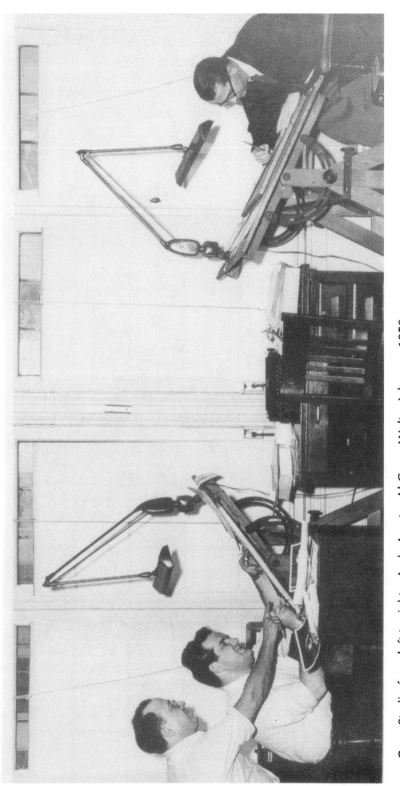

Capp Studio from left to right—Andy Amato, Al Capp, Walter Johnson, 1950.

Capp Studio—from left to right—Walter Johnson, Andy Amato, Al Capp, 1950.

Al Capp and his good friend Milton Caniff, in the 1950s.

TWENTY CENTS   NOVEMBER 6, 1950

TIME

THE WEEKLY NEWSMAGAZINE

AL CAPP
For an ailing ("sob!") world: Kickapoo Joy Juice.
(Press)

$6.00 A YEAR   (REG. U. S. PAT. OFF.)   VOL. LVI NO. 19

In 1950, members of the family gathered for a picture. On the sofa are Madeline Gardner, Al Capp and Ruth Caplin, Elliott Caplin's wife. Standing are Louis Garner, Elliott Caplin and Rabbi Isadore Davidsen, an uncle of the Caplins.

From left to right—Elliot Caplin, Madeline Gardner (sister), Jerry Capp (brother), 1989.

Genesis

As the mythology of "Li'l Abner" grew it developed its own momentum. Alfred believed as did Socrates, that the unexamined life is not worth living. And examining life was what Alfred wanted to do.

After the strip had become a success, Alfred felt that it needed an historian as the Trojan War needed an historian. And Alfred became his own Homer.

He built his walls and topless towers and created Dogpatch to rival, in its excesses, the story of Troy. At 16 he asked his friend, Gus, if Gus had any smokes. Gus said no, and the mythology started.

We lived in a scabrous house that mocked the genteel elegance of our neighbors. It was yet another one of Momma miracles; the rent was stunningly low even if collectable. But Momma knew all the rules of survival. Pay the first month no matter how hard it was to garner the $40 and let time and God take care of the rest.

The one disadvantage of living on Washington Place was the distance from shopping. It was four long blocks to a grocery story or a variety shop that sold cigarettes. Thus, when Gus told Alfred that no he didn't have any smokes, they started to hitchhike to the shopping area.

Between them they totaled a bankroll of $10.15. Alfred had worked a week as a replacement switchboard operator at a New Haven hospital. His inexperience and his utter contempt for mechanical objects (even as a successful artist he found it almost impossible to draw a machine) made him superfluous to the hospital's plans for excellence in the treatment of its patients. He was given $12 and told never to return unless he arrived as an accident victim.

Alfred still had $10 of the $12 and Gus had 15¢. It was the most money they had ever possessed singly or as a couple.

Almost unconsciously, as Alfred limped toward the tobacco store, he waved his thumb at passing cars. He would always prefer riding to walking. A sparkling four door sedan slowed and pulled up alongside the walkers.

"Where are you kids going?" the driver inquired.

"Depends," replied Gus.

"Well, if you want a hitch, hop in." The driver was about to continue on his way.

The boys got into the car.

"We were heading..." Al started to speak.

"I'm driving to Baltimore," the driver interrupted.

"Oh," said Alfred. He turned to Gus. "How about it?"

Gus shrugged. "Why not?"

That was the first leg on a journey that took them to Alfred's Uncle George, an orthodox Rabbi in Memphis, Tennessee.

The itinerary was at best haphazard, as were their sleeping arrangements and meals. The $10.15 was quickly invested in hamburgers, Coca-Colas and Camel cigarettes. Down to nothing, Alfred and Gus subsisted on the kindness of strangers.

The weather was warm and although sleeping outdoors had distinct disadvantages, they managed to survive. Damp, bedraggled and always hungry, they found truck drivers the most generous of all road travelers. It was rare that one of them failed to invite the obviously famished boys into a diner.

It was in the Great Smokies that Alfred and Gus had a brief brush with paradise. They had accepted a ride from a battered old Model T piloted by an uncommunicative old farmer who did nothing but spit into the wind. He didn't seem to mind that the sputum arched back and splattered Alfred and Gus with a viscous amalgam of tobacco juice and corn kernels.

Drenched and disgusted, Alfred spoke. "Would you mind dropping us off here, sir?"

The farmer pulled up, deposited his passengers, and without another word rattled off.

The boys studied the terrain. It was startlingly beautiful. About 500 feet off the road, they saw a log cabin on the crest of a gentle slope.

"I'm thirsty," Gus said.

"So am I," said Alfred.

They headed for the cabin. When no one answered their knock, they went around to the rear. And stared. They stared at a naked man and a naked woman, both in their 20s, seated on a rude bench eating sandwiches and drinking what looked like cool lemonade.

The naked man said: "Welcome to Eden, Strangers. Won't you join us?"

Trying desperately not to yawp, the travelers each enjoyed a sandwich and a cool glass of lemonade. The naked woman was a courteous hostess and packed several sandwiches for the road.

It was almost an hour later before either boy was able to speak.

"Did what happened really happen?" Gus was munching on the naked lady's sandwich.

Alfred remained thoughtfully silent.

They arrived at Uncle George's house in a middle-class section of Memphis 10 days after accepting the first ride to Baltimore.

The Baccarats greeted the pilgrims with their customary warmth. The customary warmth lasted until Alfred and Gus managed to outrage Uncle George and Aunt Minnie with their quaint toilet habits and relentless pursuit of the daughters of Uncle George's parishioners.

It was Aunt Minnie, the practical one, who ordered the boys to leave or, she said, she would kill herself.

They left and returned seven days later to Bridgeport. Momma wept and scolded Alfred simultaneously. He provided few details of the trip, but didn't stop eating or noshing between meals for weeks.

When "Li'l Abner" became a success, Alfred would resolutely maintain that the trip to Memphis was but a preliminary tour of the hillbilly country so that the future cartoonist could research the characters who wound up populating his wildly successful comic strip.

So much for Homer. So much for the Trojan War.

Class Reunion

High on the list of instruments of torture that land-mine the road to maturity is Entering a New Grammar School.

You've been enrolled by your mother in an elementary institution. Little by little, and at great expense to your self-respect, you get yourself accepted by your peers. Or ignored without being slapped around. Then the family moves and you have to go through the agony of acceptance once more. It never becomes easier, this re-admission to the vicious circle of contemporaries. Harder, is what it gets.

Each time one of Poppa's new business ventures failed, we moved, as though renewed motion via moving vans would cast a magical spell over our future and we could live in the same house until it was time to get married or get buried.

I went to eight grammar schools in eight years and have had the scars to prove it. These included a chewed left ear lobe, a bad knee that refuses to operate at peak efficiency in emergencies, a scar behind my ear and a torn tendon in my right arm. These badges of combat were inflicted by welcoming committees at Truman Avenue School, Scranton School, P.S. 182, Barnum School and the Sherwood Avenue School. That leaves about four institutions of lower learning where I seemed to have escaped unmarked. I don't believe it. I'm sure I suffered at all of them. At least, when I think back, I do so with shuddering distaste.

So when I got a letter from Abie Shulman announcing a reunion of our third grade class at Truman Grammar School, New Haven, Connecticut, I wrote back that I'd attend. Fifty years had passed since I had spent a year in Miss Condon's third grade. And I remember vividly hating her and every minute spent in that depressing, suffocating room. And still I wrote Abie that yes, I'd come to the Cheshire Country Club for the affair.

Alfred was to be the guest speaker. He had gone through the eighth grade at Truman, and his class was invited to attend the same reunion. He, too, had been unhappy there and I was most curious to see how he would handle this raising of despised memories.

My wife and I drove to the Cheshire Country Club, Cheshire, Connecticut. It was a large, modern building teeming with hundreds of

Truman alumni, all about my age but acting far more cheerful and friendly than I remembered them when they were my classmates. The reunion, I discovered, was open to all students who attended Truman in 1922. Why 1922 was a celebratory year was never explained.

Desperately, I searched for a familiar face. Even for a remotely recognizable feature. None showed. I, however, felt more relaxed than I thought feasible because nobody in that noisy crowd of celebrants tried to chew off the lobe of my left ear or pull my right arm out of its socket. Age can mellow, I decided.

Abie Shulman, my boyhood friend who had written to invite me to the reunion, was not there. At least I couldn't find him. There were faces that began to emerge which transcended anonymity and vibrated in my memory box; a nose that tilted exactly the way it tilted back in the Miss Condon days; or a prognathous jaw that omened a rough tussle in the toilet with Fred Thompson, whose only joy in life was in creating some form of torture he hoped I would not endure.

But I couldn't be sure, and in the din and happy confusion of this gathering it was impossible to hold normal conversation. Besides which, I brooded, what could I say to Miss Tilt Nose? I couldn't articulate in her presence 50 years ago and I feel the same now. And Fred Thompson? Frankly, I was afraid that if I confronted him he might urinate on me as he frequently did back in the third grade at Truman.

And then, like a traveler debarking at a latitude in the Arctic Circle where the glory of the lights of aurora borealis become visible, I spotted Georgie Balotin!

I had mounted a raised platform to be able to see over the heads of the massed guests and find the lost Abie Shulman. The bodies of the swarming multitude were cuddled, torso against torso in tiers that reached from the frontal edge of the dance floor to the rear brace of windows.

Row by row I searched the faces. No Abie Shulman. No anybody who looked familiar. And then I focused, or tried to focus, on a pair of eyes that looked upwards at me with the glistening reverence of a peasant girl about to hold a dialogue with the Virgin Mary. It was Georgie Balotin! It was a case of instant—no delay, but—instant recognition!

Why? Because although Georgie Balotin had two eyes, one looked straight at you while the other eye wandered off in whimsical disregard to the laws of focus, whatever they are. George Balotin was cockeyed.

Georgie Balotin had been cockeyed as a kid and had obviously decided to remain that way—at least for 50 years. I had always liked

George, and had gotten quite used to his wayward eye.

And cockeyed people look the same all their lives. If not the same, then utterly distinctive. There was no doubt about it. I had found one friend from my third grade.

Georgie and I embraced. The passage of half century had not addled his brain or dimmed his enthusiasm, even when enthusiasm was superfluous or embarrassing.

"How did you recognize me?" I asked my old friend.

"Easy," Georgie answered. "Abie Schulman told me you were coming so I was on the lookout for you."

"Great!" I pounded Georgie's arm and he pounded mine.

Reunions can be hell on upper arms.

"How did you recognize me?" Georgie queried, still pounding my arm.

Although I knew the question was coming, I curdled in dismay. What was I going to say to this warm and affectionate man? "Because kids who were cockeyed as kids always look the same when they grow up!" It was unthinkable.

I said, trying to look him straight in the eye and finding it impossible, "Because you haven't changed that much, Georgie. You still have a good head of hair (indeed he had!) and you sound the way you always did. I mean, cheerful. That kind of thing..."

Georgie smiled. "That's what everybody says." He paused, searching the room. He stiffened in excitement. "He's here," he shouted. "Al's here!"

My brother had arrived and was instantly surrounded by a mob of adoring Truman School graduates. He nodded and smiled, and signed autographs, and then looked up, saw me, and grinned and stared.

"Georgie Balotin!" he yelled.

Georgie Balotin froze in an ecstasy of instant celebrity.

"Al, Al," he chanted in a mantra of adoration. He moved toward my brother, both of his eyes phosphorescent with rapture.

Alfred reached out to grasp one of Georgie's outstretched hands.

"For God's sake, Al," Georgie panted. "How did you recognize me?"

Alfred answered, "Because you were a cockeyed kid and cockeyed kids grow up looking exactly the way they did when they were very young. You haven't changed a bit, Georgie."

Georgie Balotin smiled with infinite pleasure.

Alfred continued. "I always loved the way you looked, Georgie. I mean, you were unique. Distinctive."

Georgie nodded in an ecstasy of agreement. "That's why I never had it fixed." He pointed to his perverse eye. "People always said that it was an easy operation. But I said no. No. I didn't want it fixed, Al. And you know why? I had the feeling you'd know why. Better than anybody, you'd know why."

Alfred knew why. I don't know how he knew. But he did.

Georgie asked for two autographs. One for himself and one for his son.

Al and Dick

When the Watergate investigation began to dribble into our lives, it grew from a rivulet into a torrent of hate and indignation. And consummate curiosity.

How much did President Nixon know about the shabby little cabal of plotters holed up in the White House basement? What information about the raid on the Democratic Committee office was revealed to our Chief executive? Each time a witness spoke, more than half the ears of America were listening. It was the greatest, most exciting, utterly revealing show in the history of television.

And the question persisted. What was Richard Nixon's participation and knowledge of these squalid goings-on?

Nixon had discovered Al Capp as a kindred spirit. "Li'l Abner" has veered from its liberal stance to one of frequent and often acerbic criticism of what Alfred called, "liberal frauds." Never actually political in his attitudes, Alfred attacked fakery and humbug wherever he found it. And in the last few years of his life, he aimed his satire at the counterfeit heroes of the left. Richard Nixon felt a warm and deep kinship as a result and invited Alfred and Catherine to a prayer breakfast at the White House.

It had been ordained, at least during the Nixon years, that prayer breakfasts start early. Diabolically early. Alfred griped at the unearthly hour of the sanctified rendezvous, and was all for forgetting about it and ordering breakfast in his room. Alfred, like many others, could not function as a practicing human being without his morning mouthful of scalding coffee. More than prayer of sanctification or forgiveness, he craved his caffeine.

Passionately unhappy, Alfred permitted Catherine to herd him into a taxi. All during the ride to the White House, he griped and threatened. Catherine remained calm, gracious and soothing. She got her husband into the Lincoln room shortly before 8 a.m.

Feeling deprived, forlorn and discriminated against, Alfred sulked, hunched uncomfortably on a red brocade chair Mary Todd had, according to legend, once ripped in a pique.

Catherine stood beside him, murmuring consolingly.

Several splendidly attired butlers appeared, carrying trays, cups, saucers and gleaming decanters of coffee. Alfred, almost in a trance, watched the caffeine-loaded smoke escape from the spouts of the decanter. He rose and mumbled something to Catherine.

Catherine gasped. She knew what was about to happen. Her husband was in the grip of caffeine madness.

"Alfred! You can't! We're supposed to wait for the President!"

"You can wait." He waved his hand in a vague circle. "The others can wait. I'm going to have my coffee."

Alfred confronted a butler. "I'll have some of that," he said, motioning toward the steaming carafe.

The butler swallowed hard. "Yes, sir. How would you like your coffee?"

"Black, with a level teaspoon of sugar and a splash of milk, not cream. Milk, not cream."

He drank his coffee and smiled for the first time since his 6:30 wake-up call.

I had asked my brother if he thought Richard Nixon was alert to what was happening during the Watergate experience. He told me the story about the prayer breakfast and the coffee.

Alfred continued, "Two years after the breakfast, I was invited to the White House by Nixon. I went, and was shown into the Oval Office. The President was there with John Erlichman and Charles Colson.

"Nixon was relaxed. He could be quite charming at times. I wasn't sure why I'd been invited, but I went more out of curiosity than for any other logical reason.

"The President looked at Erlichman. 'John, you'll have Scotch on the rocks... 'Chuck'—Colson, that is—'Chuck,' he said 'you'll have your bourbon straight, I'll have my vodka and tonic' and then he turned to me, and he smiled that conspiratorial smile of his. He said, 'and Al, you'll have a cup of black coffee with a level teaspoon of sugar and a splash of milk—not cream, milk. Am I right?' "

Alfred faced me, straight faced. "And you're asking me if he knew what was going on in the White House?"

Ham Fisher: The Feud

Ham Fisher was a pudgy, articulate man with a passion for fame, money and the rapt attention of beautiful women. He had stormed the offices of the McNaught Newspaper Syndicate to sell them his comic strip, "Joe Palooka." Benign old man McNitt, the boss, ignored the rather primitive drawings of Fisher but offered him a job as syndicate salesman.

Ham Fisher accepted the offer, sold many of the McNaught standard features as well as his own creation, giving newspaper feature editors the impression that his comic strip was being distributed by McNaught. When he faced the old man McNitt with 20 clients for "Joe Palooka," the syndicate head decided the strip had possibilities.

In subsequent years, "Joe Palooka" became an outstanding comics page hit. Fisher was a clever story teller and created winning characters. That he was a less than capable artist bothered him, but he compensated by filling in the faces of main characters on the bodies drawn by more talented artists in his employ.

When Alfred was limping away from the building that housed The Daily News-Chicago Tribune syndicate, his rejected drawings in a black portfolio under his arm, he was hailed, "Hey, Kid!"

It was Ham Fisher. His sister was waiting for him in his car.

"What've you got in that portfolio, sonny?"

"What the hell is it to you?" Alfred answered.

"Don't work up a sweat about it, kid. I bet my sister," Fisher motioned to the woman in the car, "that you were just tossed out of the syndicate office. Am I right?"

He was right. Alfred showed Fisher his work and was hired to "ink" Ham's drawings. Only the creator of "Joe Palooka" did no more than indicate action with stick figures. Alfred discovered that inking meant pencilling as well. But he was satisfied. He was working and learning—and making money.

The money wasn't much. Alfred's starting salary was $25 a week. He brought Catherine and his infant daughter, Julie, to New York and found a one-room flat on W. 91st Street, off Central Park West.

The salary left little room for luxuries, since Alfred was spending several dollars a week to support his kid brother—me—a freshman at Ohio State University. When Alfred subtly suggested there wasn't enough light in his flat to accommodate his after-hours work on "Joe Palooka," Ham offered his assistant a lamp he had no use for. Not a raise. A lamp.

Ham, recognizing Alfred's talents, gave him free rein in his drawing of the Sunday's pages, and in the writing as well. The result was a series of zany uncharacteristic Palooka continuities that featured a huge, slow-witted hillbilly Alfred named "Big Liviticus."

After six months with Fisher, Alfred decided he had no future working for a salary that gave no sign of budging from the barest survival level. He worked steadily at home on what was to become "Li'l Abner" and sold the comic strip to United Features Syndicate.

During the first few years of Abner's career, Ham Fisher was friendly and encouraging the few times he talked to Alfred. When the strip began to reach the new heights it did in its fifth year, outdistancing "Joe Palooka" in a number of papers as well as in the esteem of the cartooning fraternity, Fisher altered his stance. He boasted that Al Capp had created "Li'l Abner" while in his employ, suggesting it was his generous patronage that laid the foundation for the strip's success. Alfred never quibbled about the obvious relationship between "Big Liviticus" and "Li'l Abner." He freely admitted that his hillbilly was germinated in the Sunday pages of "Joe Palooka."

As Abner's popularity grew and Al Capp himself became a celebrity appearing on numerous TV shows as well as in the columns of the leading weekly news magazines, Fisher's discontent blossomed into savage attacks on Alfred and his comic strip.

Lindy's restaurant had become the favorite meeting place for pastrami and chopped liver aficionados. It was here that Ham Fisher expanded and dilated his dislike for Al Capp. With an audience of well-known literary figures, theatre luminaries, newspaper columnists and cartoonists, Fisher would flatly accuse Capp of arrogant plagiarism. And more.

Alfred never responded verbally. Instead, he wrote a short story for *The Atlantic Monthly* entitled "I Remember Monster," in which he catalogued with destructive detail the "imaginary" travails of a young artist laboring for a successful but woefully stingy artist. No one doubted for a moment who "monster" was. Ham fumed and threatened, but even his friends were amused by Alfred's portrayal.

The feud grew and flourished. Ham Fisher's assaults on Alfred occurred with feverish intensity; it seemed to dominate his life and infect all of his social relationships. He discarded and camouflaged amiability, and flatly accused Al Capp of thievery (no longer "plagiarism") and passionately urged that his ex-protege should be banished from the surface of the earth.

The effect of this quarrel had grown insidiously. Still, my own relationship with Fisher had managed to survive to the point where he would answer my telephone call with a friendly, "Hey, kiddo—how're you doing?"

I had phoned Fisher to discuss the growing dimension of the ugly skirmishes that now were troubling my brother probably as much as they were infecting Ham. We agreed to meet and talk at five o'clock at the Biltmore Hotel's popular men's bar.

Arriving first, I managed to take possession of a booth in the crowded, noisy bar. Fisher arrived, panting, and searching in the jammed room. Spotting me, he waved. I beckoned him toward the booth I had held against threatening threesomes and foursomes.

Fisher waved me toward the swarming bar where drinkers were dovetailed, elbow to elbow. Sighing, I relinquished my embattled hold on the precious booth and followed Fisher as he galloped around the bar, trying to find space for our two bodies.

Abruptly he halted and flagged me toward a slot barely large enough to accommodate one body; Ham maneuvered his chunky torso into the opening, wedging my yielding body next to him so that I was almost tattooed to the chest of a large and, I thought, threatening, man on my left.

We ordered drinks. Ham was smiling affably. "What's on your mind, kiddo?"

"You know what's on my mind, Ham."

"You mean that son of a bitch of a crook?" He meant my brother.

"This insanity has to stop, Ham." I thought I kept my temper admirably.

Fisher shrugged, wedging me tighter against the large threatening man on my left. "So what happens if I don't stop blowing the whistle on that rat fink brother of yours?"

"We'll kill you, Ham." What I meant was perfectly clear to me and Fisher. Our side would fight back with all the energy at our disposal to make Ham out to be the vindictive paranoiac I was now quite certain he was.

We parted with strained amiability. I felt I had accomplished nothing of any consequence.

A month passed and I walked into the lobby of the Statler Hotel in Washington, D.C. A publishing function involving newspaper syndicates, cartoonists, editors, writers and publishers was being held there.

In the center of the lobby a group of newspaper people were clustered around Ham Fisher. When one of them recognized me, he nudged Fisher, who looked up, saw me and stopped talking. I went to my room and began to unpack, sensing direction and import of Ham Fisher's lobby discourse. It was a disturbing thought.

Because of the overflow attendance for this meeting, hotel rooms were being shared. I discovered when he entered with his own key that my roommate was Harry Gilbert, Sales Manager for United Features.

After a brief greeting, Harry studied me with a mixture of compassion and inquisitive concern. "Fisher got you good, didn't he?"

"He got me? How? How did Fisher get me, Harry?"

"At the bar. The Biltmore men's bar." Harry ran his words together. He was hungry for more detail.

Genuinely confused, I replied, "I met Fisher at the Biltmore but did you say he got me at the men's bar?"

Harry studied me with the intensity of a lab clinician hunched over a rare specimen. He must have decided that my confusion was genuine.

"Do you remember standing at the bar?"

"Of course I do. Fisher wouldn't come to the booth I had and insisted on stuffing both our bodies into the mob at the bar."

"A-huh," Harry nodded. "And do you recall who you were stuffed next to...at the bar, I mean?"

I pondered. "No...not exactly...who remembers who's next to him at a bar, anyway. Why do you ask?"

Harry rose and approached me. He placed a sympathetic hand on my shoulder, like a friendly District Attorney might to a cooperative witness. "And did you threaten Ham's life?"

"What the hell are you talking about—did I threaten Ham's life!"

"Ham said—down in the lobby no more than 10 minutes ago—that you said you'd kill him if he didn't stop picking on your brother."

A gasp was the best I could do. "Yes, I said we'd kill him...but I didn't mean...terminate him. Not kill him literally.... He knew that. It was only...you know...an expression...We all say it...a hundred times a day. You know—" Now I was sputtering.

"Well," Harry continued relentlessly. "When you made that death threat you did it in the presence of a policeman—a private detective and one other witness—"

Now I gasped for real. The large and threatening man on my left! And the man he was talking to! How did Fisher get them down to the men's bar so fast? I didn't doubt for a moment he had managed it.

There was no sense in telling Alfred of the incident. It was highly unlikely that Fisher would hail me into court on a murder threat charge. Unless, of course, it might cause my brother some suffering. This possibility bothered me. No malice was beyond Ham's state-of-the-art vengeance.

Before I could reason out some defense against the chance that Fisher might strike at Alfred through me, the State of New York appointed a commission to investigate the baleful influences on the youth of America of the burgeoning comic book business; as a footnote to this exploration of literary child abuse, the commission was instructed also to explore questionable practices in syndicated comic strips.

"Li'l Abner" became a prime target for the Commission. Although Alfred himself was never questioned, the committee published a report containing several panels from the comic strip purporting to show that the cartoonist had deliberately drawn phallic symbols in an effort to corrupt and titillate his young readers.

Although "Li'l Abner" often hinted gleefully that women could be luscious and desirable and that men could be wantonly lustful, it was always done in a mood of hilarious exaggeration so that the conclusion that men and women often panted in expectation would come as no surprise to anybody.

The reproductions of the original drawings by Al Capp, reproduced in the Commission report, were undoubtedly taken from the daily strip. Only there was something oddly disarranged in the proportions. The strips for which the mats were made and provided to the client newspapers were not immediately available. And Alfred was wildly impatient to discover who had tampered with the drawings.

Through his lawyers, Greenbaum Wolff and Ernst, an ex-FBI man was hired. In a miraculously short span of time he managed to obtain the anonymous letters that had been sent to the Commission. Under close examination it became immediately evident that someone had tampered with the "Li'l Abner" drawings, adding a line here, a shadow there, resulting in body parts that did actually look phallic. Using mysteriously puzzling machines, the ex-FBI man showed us where each emendation had taken place.

In addition to proving that Alfred's originals had been doctored, the FBI man was able to prove that the hand scrawls adjacent to the tainted drawings belonged to, and there was no surprise here, Ham Fisher.

It would serve no purpose to publicize this fraud, we decided. And an apology from the New York State Commission was not high on our list of priorities. What would Alfred do with it? It was certainly weak material for an Abner continuity. And there were no villains to speak of. Only politicians who hadn't bothered to check their copy.

And of course there was Ham. But Ham was sick. Seriously ill with cancer.

The mildest reproof we could come up with was to report our findings to the National Cartoonists Society. This group represented practically every cartoonist in the nation, and was highly respected by its membership. Ham Fisher regarded the opinion of his peers probably the most important judgment of his life.

The committee of his colleagues found Fisher guilty of fraud and fakery and cast him from the society.

Ham Fisher went to the studio of his assistant and took his own life.

There was no sense of retribution. Only sadness.

The Return of O.P. Caplin

When Momma died, Alfred phoned my father. He was living in a Chicago suburb. Aunt Rose, my father's sister, provided his address. We all listened to the conversation.

Alfred: Hello, Pa.
Papa: Alfred?
Alfred: Yes, Pa...Momma died today.
Papa: Oh. I'm sorry.
Alfred: The funeral is tomorrow.
Papa: I see.
(Pause).
Alfred: Will you be coming to it?
Papa: The funeral?
Alfred: Yes.
Papa: I guess you don't know.
Alfred: What?
Papa: Your mother and I were divorced.
Alfred: Oh. When?
Papa: Almost 12 years ago.
(Pause)
Alfred: Does that mean you won't be coming?
Papa: I don't think it would serve any purpose.
Alfred: I see.
Papa: I'm married.
Alfred: Married?
Papa: Yes. I remarried almost 10 years ago.

Papa didn't come to the funeral. But he did come back into our lives.

Fathers, of course, are never young. So when Otto Caplin arrived in New York with his wife, Edna, there was no significant change in his appearance. His clothes were fashionable and his manner affable. Edna, however, was something of a surprise. She was about as different from

77

Mama as a woman could be. I suppose that really means that to me she was deeply and permanently gentile even to her hair frizzled into unbecoming ringlets that peeped out from the helmet-like cloche she was wearing.

Oddly, there was no resentment on the part of his sons to his marriage. Madeline, however, remained steadfast in her stern attitude toward my father and his new wife.

Papa returned to Chicago and a correspondence began. He had always been a prodigious writer, even during the years when he traveled the Midwest and returned home rarely. He suggested that he was clearly in need of financial support and unabashedly recommended a salary of $100 a week. Alfred, Bence and I agreed, and Poppa became my publishing representative in the Chicago area. Somewhat to my surprise, he proved conscientious and devoted to his job.

A year passed, during which Poppa submitted his field reports to me regularly. He also informed us that he had enrolled in an extension program at the University of Chicago and was completing a course in creative writing. He wrote, "I've finished the first draft of my autobiography and I must say with no modesty whatsoever that it's quite good. Good enough, I think, to be published."

The manuscript arrived, neatly typed by Edna, an experienced typist and secretary. I scarcely glanced at it, but phoned Jack Goodman, an executive at Simon and Schuster and a friend of mine.

"Jack, I've got a favor to ask of you."
"Naturally. What is it?"
"My father has written a book."
Jack Goodman groaned.
"Will you read it and let him down easy? He's not a young man."
Jack Goodman groaned again, louder than before. "Send the pile of shit to me." He hung up.
A month passed. Papa phoned.

Papa: I'm coming to New York.
Me: Oh. Great. Any special reason, Pa?
Papa: I heard from that friend of yours. The publisher.
Me: The publisher?
Papa: (Impatiently) Of course. The one at that company. The Simon and something company.

Me: Oh. You mean Simon and Schuster.

Papa: That's the one.

Me: And?

Papa: They want it.

Me: (Stupidly) It?

Papa: The book!

Me: Oh. The book. Of course. Jack Goodman.

Papa: That's the one.

Me: (Carefully) He...ah...I mean...

Papa: He wrote that he wants my book. I just told you that.

Me: Wants! Why, Pa, that's terrific. Wonderful. Look...can I call you right back. Got another call waiting. Right back!

Feverishly, I phoned Jack Goodman.

"Jack, I just heard from my father. He says you want to publish his autobiography?

"He's out of his mind. And you're out of your mind. Publish that pile of crap?"

"But Jack, he's coming to New York. He says you wrote him..."

"Of course I wrote him."

"And did you give him the impression that you were buying the book?"

Jack Goodman groaned as it seemed he did any time we had a conversation.

"You told me to let the old man down easy."

"Christ, not that easy!" I hung up.

My father picked up the phone on the first ring.

Me: Look, Pa. About Simon and Schuster...

Papa: You mean my publishers.

Me: Yes. Well...you see...

Papa: See what?

Me: There's a rumor making the rounds.

Papa: What kind of rumor?

Me: It's not a good rumor, Pa. Not at all.

Papa: What in the Sam Hill are you talking about, Bence?

(Note: My father always had trouble identifying me. Frequently, he thought I was my brother Bence. I had gotten quite used to it.)

Me: Well, the word around town is that Simon and Schuster are...well, to put it bluntly...barely hanging on...publishing wise.

Papa: You mean to tell me you had me send my manuscript to a fly-by-night bunch of phonies?

Me: Well, they weren't always like that, Pa. As a matter of fact, in the past...

Papa: (Coldly) I'm not interested in the past, Bence.

Me: Look, Pa. Don't worry. I know some other publishers...

Papa: (Bitterly) Are these publishers in business on a more permanent basis?

Me: Definitely, Pa. I'll get the manuscript back and send it to...to...

Papa: Yes?

Me: Prentice Hall! That's it. Prentice Hall.

Papa: I've never heard of them.

Me: They're first rate, Pa.

I sent my father's book to Prentice Hall and they decided to publish it. My father took their acceptance as a matter of course and came to New York to sign the contract.

Before he completed the re-writes suggested by his editor, Poppa died. The book was never published.

Mrs. Mulrooney and the Private Parts

Andy Amato probably had as much ability as Michelangelo, but was born out of time. No one, at least in the greater Boston area, needed a ceiling painted. Thus, Andy Amato poured all his considerable talent into "Li'l Abner" as Al Capp's chief assistant.

Hawk-nosed and perpetually untidy, Andy smoked cheap cigars and giggled infectiously most of the working day. Terribly near-sighted, he wore thick-lensed glasses, and, when bent over his drawing board, his nose almost invaded the drawing he was fashioning.

Walter Johnson was assistant number two. He specialized in mechanical objects. He was as sober as Andy was manic; precision, proportion and convincing accuracy marked his contributions to the comic strip. Alfred could not draw a convincing mechanical object himself and relied on Walter to construct authentic vehicles, lathes, gears, appliances, riggings, harnesses, pedals, knobs or handspikes.

Harvey Curtis completed the task force. Laconic and distrustful of all descendants of Adam, he lived a solitary life with his ailing mother; Harvey had few friends, but many interests. Among those interests was an almost morbid fascination with guns. Alfred was never to discover whether Harvey actually fired a gun.

"If he does," Andy once confided to Alfred, "my feeling is it will be at you. Between the eyes."

Alfred agreed.

Harvey's job was to put in the blacks and letter the dialogue. The dialogue as designed by Alfred was an important integral part of the comic strip. Harvey was superb in mirroring in his lettering the actions and mood of the characters.

"Li'l Abner" was truly an ensemble effort. The story sessions were often romps through the wildest fantasies of the four men. Each brought to the studio his own prodigal dreams and tried to flesh out his urges, prejudices, hang ups in an Abner continuity.

"How about" was the kick-off for a story conference.

"How about this guy who's never been to a city bigger than like a couple of hundred people...how about him coming to the big city...New

81

York or Boston...and looking for a girl whose picture he's seen let's say on the cover of...let's see...maybe not on a magazine but on a poster like a Nehi poster...and..."

That was Andy Amato launching. Harvey would break in: "How about the girl is a man in drag? It has vast possibilities."

Andy huffed. "None of that aberrational shit," he warned.

"Wait a minute," Alfred interjected. "Harvey may have something there."

"Yeah," Walter Johnson offered, "irreparable brain damage."

Alfred continued, "Abner sees the poster...it shows the beautiful figure of a girl...great body...fantastic legs...only...only the poster had been ripped..."

"The face is missing!" And yelled, in delighted.

"Right!"

The four men would explore and dissect the story line. A hundred variations were discussed and discarded. Time would pass, and eventually a continuity was fashioned that could be a hundred years away from an original concept.

Alfred appreciated and rewarded his staff. He especially valued Andy for his unorthodox and undisciplined flights into absolute insanity. Andy Amato felt free to soar, knowing that Alfred would exercise his superb story sense in fashioning the final drawn version of Andy's frequent bouts with paranoia.

Entering the studio, you had the unmistakable feeling that you weren't visiting, you were being admitted. Artists at work have a distinct and peculiar odor. They reek, it is true, with sweaty effort but the scent is laced with a perfume that only creativity can produce. Alfred's studio radiated this aroma of Promethian rapport. It made a visitor feel somewhat freakish.

Each of the four men had a long rectangular mirror hung over his drawing board. Frequently, one would glance upwards into the looking glass and make a face so grotesque it could frighten an unsuspecting visitor. Studying the face, the artist would than transfer the mirrored expression to paper. I could not look at any Abner character without seeing Alfred or Andy or Walter in one or more features in the drawing.

I loved to visit the studio. It boasted a comfortable couch and I would spend the night there, having hitch-hiked from New York, where I was living with my mother shortly before my marriage.

The first time I spent the night at the studio, I rested comfortably and rose in the morning to dress and shave. While shaving, I heard the studio door being unlocked and opened. I waited for Alfred or Andy, Walter, or Harvey.

Instead, there was a whispering silence. It sounded like somebody was wiping or dusting with the delicacy of a an artist. Indeed, it was something like dusting. It was Mrs. Mulroney, the cleaning lady.

Intent on her dusting, Mrs. Mulroney was obviously avoiding me. She barely glanced in my direction when I peeked out of the bathroom, razor in hand, face covered with lather, and greeted her.

It took me about 20 minutes to finish the shaving procedure. During this time, concentrating on my mirror image, I became aware of Mrs. Mulroney peering at me furtively through the half-opened bathroom door. When I glanced in her direction, the cleaning lady would scurry away, her dust cloth extended like a lancer's pennant. It was a puzzling affair, but I decided the peculiarities of Mrs. Mulroney were really none of my business.

I left Boston that morning without seeing Alfred. About three months passed and I revisited the studio. The men, who were hard at work, nodded greeting and returned to the drawing board. I wandered around and stopped in the corner adjacent to the bathroom to ponder a hatbox sitting on a low able. It was covered with dust in contrast to the polished surfaces of the other pieces of furniture in that room. On the dust-laden cover of the hatbox was a hand-lettered message. It read: "Elliott's Private Parts."

Alfred, Andy, Walter and Harvey were watching me with expressions of suspended exultation; their pens were poised mid-air over their drawing boards. Whatever it was that had happened they had fashioned as they plotted a "Li'l Abner" continuity. And I was the goat. Or hero. Only time would tell.

Wordlessly, I pointed to the dust-covered box with its chilling legend: "Elliott's Private Parts."

As though I was a bell-ringing Pavlov, the men began to laugh as soon as I pointed to the hat box. Alfred had broken first; his guffaw developed into a roar of exuberant laughter. His pen fell to the floor as he bent double in joyous contortions.

Andy removed his thick-lensed glasses to wipe his tearing eyes. Walter was grimacing in a silent spasm of joy. Even Harvey's guarded misanthropic chuckle managed to sound jubilant. Obviously, I was the butt of the joke. But what the hell was the joke?

"What the hell is the joke?" I asked the funny four. It was Harvey who recovered first. Readjusting his customary scowl, he explained. All during the exposition, the others continued to snort, giggle and grow weak with explosions of laughter.

Harvey told me: "When you were here at the studio last time, we phoned Mrs. Mulroney."

"The cleaning woman?" I queried.

"The same," Harvey continued. "We told her that Al's kid brother was spending the night and that you were only dangerous."

"Dangerous!" I shouted.

"Dangerous," Harvey continued ignoring my passionate outburst, "only when you were shaving. We convinced her that otherwise gentle and docile, with a shaving razor in your hand you became a self-destructive maniac."

I admit I was enthralled. "Yes. Go on, Harvey."

"With a razor in your grip you could be counted on to either slit your throat..."

"My God," I shuddered.

"Or," Harvey continued relentlessly, "any other part of your body you were temporarily discontented with."

Appalled, I studied the dusty hat box.

"And..." I was trembling.

"Naturally," Harvey went on inexorably, "we convinced Mrs. Mulroney that your brother's loyalty and devotion..."

"Loyalty! Devotion!"

"Loyalty and devotion to your memory meant that the severed parts..."

"Oh, Jesus, shut up!" The three men must have regarded my protest as immensely witty. They laughed even harder.

Harvey was on a roll, ignoring me and the others. "The severed parts were to be memorialized in that receptacle," he pointed to the hatbox, "and Mrs. Mulroney was to pay proper respect for the remains of Mr. Capp's young and once promising brother."

"Hence the dust?" I was calming down now.

"Hence the dust. Mrs. Mulroney wouldn't touch your private parts with a ten-foot pole."

Small wonder.

The Norman Rockwell Collection

The war was over and like a couple of million other young men and women, I was anxious to forget it ever happened. Now a civilian, I found that the texture of life had changed during my service, but not the tensions. I had my old job back, but something decidedly new had been added—a baby son.

With a child in the house, inarticulate but never the less dictatorial, my wife and I grimly resolved to raise the kid and any potential brothers or sisters in the suburbs. Or at least a distance away from the neighborhoods that might endanger their health or stunt their growth.

It was Alfred who came to the rescue. "Why don't we do a comic strip together? We'll split the writers' share—that ought to pay for a house for you and your family."

Al Capp had already achieved renown. It was an established fact that his name on a comic strip made it instantly salable. I was most enthusiastic about collaborating with him.

"But will you have time to draw another strip?"

"Who said I was going to draw it?" Alfred replied.

"But who..."

"Who?" Alfred smiled. "Who's the best known artist in the U.S.? Maybe in the world?"

I thought. "You can't mean...?

"Of course I do."

Was it possible. "You're suggesting...Norman Rockwell?"

"Naturally," Al responded briskly. "Get in touch with him and get his reaction."

"How much can I say he'll be paid?" Even talented artists are avid collectors of financial data like salaries and percentages.

Alfred pondered. "Go to King Features. See what they'll guarantee Rockwell and us."

I went to King Features, largest of all syndicates and the richest. Joe Connelly, head of the organization, was guardedly enthusiastic.

"Capp writing and Rockwell drawing?" He pursed his lips, leaned back in his chair and studied the immense proportions of his office as though it was his first time there. "I'd go to a thousand a week."

A thousand bucks a week! It was an unheard-of guarantee those days. A new strip might rate a couple of hundred weekly guarantee, but a thousand! Unbelievable!

Now to sound out Norman Rockwell. I phoned him in Arlington, Vermont, where he lived and worked. His voice was surprisingly high-pitched, but nonetheless cordial.

"Do a comic strip with Al Capp? What a wonderful idea," he shrilled.

It was done! With Al Capp and Norman Rockwell as my collaborator, I could not only afford a house in the suburbs, I might even furnish it.

In the following weeks I worked with my brother on the first two weeks of "Broadway Bill," our new feature. The main character was fashioned to Rockwell's talents; Bill was a country boy who made it to the big city but never lost his rural charm, his country boy awkwardness. A perfect Norman Rockwell type, we reasoned.

As thrilled as I was at the bright future that colored my every thought and move, I had enough prejudice against the fickleness of fate not to sacrifice a regular income no matter how glittering my prospects seemed to be.

My job on the editorial staff of *Parents* magazine allowed me enough time to meet with Alfred during lunch on Broadway Bill, and to leave my office at about 5:30 for my daily squash game. Quite often I played with Al Dorne, a most successful magazine illustrator and the co-founder of "The Famous Artists School," a thriving mail order art instruction business. Dorne was a massive man, stern competitor and acknowledged friend and confidante of famous artists.

"I hear," he said to me between games, "that you're doing something with Normie."

"Normie?" My pulse rate increased. I suspected something. Maybe something awful.

Dorne grinned with amiable reproach. "Don't play dumb, Caplin. I mean Normie Rockwell."

"What about Norman Rockwell?"

Al Dorne laughed. It was more a whoop than a laugh. And with good reason.

"Look." He had become serious. "It takes Normie a week to draw a finger nail. A week! You get it? The man's the most—I mean the most—meticulous craftsman since Michelangelo. And you want this guy—who takes a week to draw a fingernail—you expect him to complete 30 or 40 finished drawings for your comic strip every week of his life? If you do, you're stark raving mad. He can't do it. Even if he wanted to —impossible! Out of the question!" He shook his head tragically. "Christ. Imagine Normie finishing 30 or 40 drawings every week."

In that instant, I changed my mind about Al Dorne. It was more than apparent that this genial outgoing man was a spiteful truculent rival, malignantly jealous of the fame and fortune I and my brother were about to bestow on a colleague. How could I have ever thought of him as a good friend, a benign squash buddy?

Rockwell had invited me and my wife to his home in Vermont. Not that I needed any reaffirmation of my verbal pact with him, I nevertheless decided to confirm the October date by phone. And I might, casually, mind you, recount with admirable restraint, my experience with the spiteful Al Dorne. After all, it was only a phone call.

"Great to hear from you," Norman exclaimed with his traditional warmth.

"I had a long talk with Al Dorne the other day, Norman."

"Oh, how lovely. A fine man, Albert. One of the best." How little he knew of the nature of the man.

"One of the best," I did my best to conceal my insincerity.

"The best," Norman concluded.

"You know what he said to me, Norman?" I tried to keep it light. It came out heavy. Only Norman didn't seem to notice. "Al Dorne said you couldn't possibly do the comic strip." I guffawed. At least a guffaw was my intent.

"What comic strip?" Norman Rockwell said.

The premonition that had been stalking me relentlessly ever since the squash experience with Al Dorne began to blossom with hideous malevolence.

" 'Broadway Bill.' You know, the comic strip my brother and I are writing and you're drawing." I felt the fool repeating what I had assumed to be facts graven on Rockwell's brain as they were on mine.

"Oh yes, of course." Rockwell seemed truly penitent. "For the moment I had forgotten."

He seemed to be waiting for me to continue our conversation.

"Well?" I continued.

"Yes?" Rockwell was politely expectant.

"Well, was he—I mean Al Dorne. You remember what I just said? I mean what Al Dorne had said?"

"Oh, Al Dorne. About my doing that—what did you say the name of it was?"

I was slowly dying. Visions of my unbought suburban house began to fade. " 'Broadway Bill.' The strip that King Features is guaranteeing us $1,000 a week. That one." Maybe he had forgotten about the thousand per. Maybe. I doubted it.

"That is an impressive amount of money." Rockwell was more polite than aroused.

In one last un-approved gambit I blurted, "And it all—the whole thousand bucks—goes to you." I didn't even bother to imagine what my brother would say to this outright grant of all profits to someone other than the Caplin brothers.

"How nice. But I couldn't possibly draw your comic strip."

" 'Broadway Bill'?"

" 'Broadway Bill.' It certainly is a catchy name," Rockwell commented.

My voice was hardly above a tortured whisper.

"Then why..."

"I can't hear you," Rockwell complained.

"I was wondering why," I had managed to become audible, "why you invited me and my wife to your home in Vermont, Norman." Why if not to discuss our mutual venture? What other earthly reason could there be to drive over 300 miles in questionable mid-October weather?

"Oh," Rockwell was exuberant. "I thought you and your wife would enjoy the boliage."

I meditated. Hard. Nothing came through. "What's a boliage, Norman?"

Norman laughed. "Not boliage, Mr. Caplin, but foliage. This is the time of the year when the foliage is at its very best. Beautiful. Really stunning. I'm sure you and Mrs. Caplin would find it thrilling."

"The foliage?"

"Just enchanting," Rockwell was carried away.

I was in control of myself. Or in control of what was left of the former comic strip potentate with the $1,000 per week guarantee from the largest syndicate in the world. I said, "Our plans have changed, Norman. Perhaps next year."

"Any time you choose, Mr. Caplin. Anytime at all."

That was the last conversation I had with Norman Rockwell.

Although I reframed my evaluation of Albert Dorne, I never played squash with him again. The memories he would have stirred in me might well have been too painful to sustain.

Alfred accepted Rockwell's decision cheerfully. I never managed more than a mournful accommodation to my shattered suburban dream.

Bravo Brazil!

Dwight David Eisenhower, yet another smalltown boy who made it to the White House, was generally considered to be an uninspired President, even a lazy one. Many felt he had amassed such a huge reservoir of war honors that there was nothing special he had to do to rate at least a footnote in history.

Almost all we remember about this genial man with the enticing smile was his lassitude through two terms as President. We forget that in his own laid-back super self-confident way (to all outward appearances, anyway,) he managed to get quite a bit done. We forget that "Ike" kept his government out of labor squabbles, reorganized the defense system, sped the end of the bloody Korean mess, endorsed the SE Asia treaties, backed the UN in scolding the French and British for their unseemly raids on Egypt.

And Eisenhower did a lot more; nothing particularly dramatic, but America didn't yearn for the dramatic during those years. They wanted a benevolent smiling uncle, and Dwight Eisenhower fit the bill to his last shining incisor.

And he formed the "People to People" Committee. This was a laudable plan to bring together in amiable conclave the peoples of the world—even the winners and losers of gory World War II into a sanguine relationship based on a mutuality of interest in their given professions. Alfred was selected to head the People to People's Cartoonists Committee. Cartoonists consider themselves the most select and selective of all creative people. Newspaper cartoonists, that is. Of all art forms, a daily and Sunday comic strip makes demands of the creator that would make the decoration of the Sistine Chapel the backyard Jungle Gym of acrobatic excellence.

It was the job of the Cartoonists Committee to break down the barriers of reinforced self-esteem that protected one comic strip or editorial cartoonist from possible unflattering comparison with a brother artist.

The State Department came to Alfred's rescue. Eager to please the President, the Foggy Bottom experts set about gathering cartoonists from all over the world to convene in the United States. Convene they did at our government's expense and with Al Capp as host in his New York apartment in the high rent district of Park Avenue.

The first batch of foreign cartoonists came from Brazil, Argentina, Columbia, Peru, Venezuela, and numbered about 20. They were uniformly handsome, dark and utterly outgoing. And absolutely unable to communicate in any language save Spanish or Portuguese.

State Department experts, slickly efficient at ordering food and drink, were quite helpless when it came to interpreting. Not a single one of the four Department aides assigned to the Al Capp welcoming party spoke a word of our guests' languages.

Alfred had invited among others the talented Walt Kelly, creator of "Pogo." Walt ably concealed his wild iconoclasm with a laconic verbal style in contrast to Alfred's vocal exuberance. I had been called to help where I could and spent most of my hour at the apartment grinning and making incomprehensible signs with my hands indicating anything from, "Would you like another drink?" to "How are things in Rio (Lima, Buenos Aires, etc.") With a tolerance that boded well for international amity, the South American cartoonists smiled and pretended that I did not at all look and sound like an idiot. The combination of continuous grinning and inchoate sign language began to pall. I slumped into a chair and observed that the South Americans were enjoying each other and gradually managed to congeal into groups that excluded most of their American colleagues. The State Department people were concentrating on hovering; they hovered on the fringes of the foreign conclaves like obsequious waiters waiting for a gratuity. Alfred was telegraphing his restlessness; his smile had frozen into a disquieting grimace, as though he were doing his damnedest to gut out a toothache. Walt Kelly, on the other hand, seemed, amazingly, to be enjoying himself. He was surrounded by the Latins and in a mysterious way seemed to be communicating without using his hands or a word of Spanish or Portuguese. It was then that my brother signaled to me with a nod of the head. We rendezvoused in the bedroom.

"Have you noticed," he said, "how much Walt Kelly is enjoying himself?"

I had noticed. "What do you intend doing about this?"

Alfred responded as he reached for his coat. "I'm getting the hell out of here. Quietly. You?"

"Quietly," I commented, reaching for my own coat.

How long the party continued I didn't find out about until several weeks later. Alfred and I were lunching.

"What happened after we left the apartment?" I asked.

Alfred regarded me grimly. "You don't know?"

"Know what? I mean, I know you sneaked out. I suppose that was a rotten thing to do to Walt Kelly. Leaving him there alone to cope with those South Americans."

"He coped." Alfred said.

There was going to be more. There had to be more. Walt Kelly continuities seldom ran less that a couple of months.

"I got back to the apartment at about 10 p.m. There was crowd of people staring up at my building. Actually, they were fascinated by the living room window in my flat."

"Any special reason?"

"Yes." Alfred responded. "There was special reason."

"Which was?"

"A baby grand piano was being lowered from my living room window. Actually, it was my baby grand piano."

"The Steinway?"

"That very one," Alfred said.

I went went on eating.

"Why was your Steinway being lowered from your living room window at 10 p.m.?"

Alfred was reflectively spearing the strawberry from the crest of the wedge of short cake. "It was the only way to get it out of the apartment—"

"But," I tried to break in. Alfred ignored me and continued eating his short cake and talking.

"The South American—I think it was the one from Buenos Aires—said that the piano had to be on board the ship before midnight. It was sailing at midnight, you see."

I could see nothing. Alfred smiled a bitter smile.

"Naturally, you want to know why a veritable stranger whose language I do not speak nor who speaks mine was transporting my baby grand piano from 715 Park Avenue to some unknown address in Argentina."

I wanted to know.

"Walt gave him the piano." He held up his hand, stopping a flood of confused questions. "Walt told the Argentinean that it was my dearest wish that he—the Argentinean—should have my Steinway. The Argentinean protested briefly, than accepted my gift with grace. The State Department man arranged for the transportation of the piano—no mean feat at that time of night—from my apartment to the Argentinean's ship."

Several minutes of silence.

Finally I said, "Why?"

"Why?" my brother mused. "Why? Well, suppose you were in his place—Walt Kelly's. You're an invited guest at somebody's house and suddenly you're the host. You're burdened with the responsibility of entertaining 30 foreigners after you've been shabbily deserted by your invitor."

"I don't know that I'd give away the piano," I ventured.

"Well, Walt Kelly did. When he called me the next day to explain I understood. Fully."

"What did he say that made you understand fully why he would contribute somebody else's valuable property without that somebody else's permission?"

"He gave me two reasons," Alfred said. "The first was it was our job as members of the People to People committee to cement relationships with our colleagues. Right?"

I was convinced. "And the second reason?"

Alfred's smile was almost angelic. "His second reason was that I can't play the piano anyway."

In the ensuing years, more parties were held, some at Alfred's apartment. None of the brother's furniture was disposed of; the only mementos of his stewardship of the People to People's Cartoonists Committee was an empty space in the north corner of the living room at 715 Park Avenue and numerous cigarette burns on the coffee and end tables.

The Prince's Secret

I have never seen Alfred contemplative without a pen or pencil in his hand. Even in his most disconsolate moments he telegraphed an excitement, a sense of anticipation, that no matter how discouraged, wretched or hopeless he might feel at any given moment, there was bound to be something wonderful—or at least challenging—around the next turn.

But now he had become thoughtful. Contemplative. And without a drawing utensil in his grip.

"I'm giving up the strip."

There was nothing I could say. Change his mind? Why should I even try? "Li'l Abner" had been so much a part of his life. Forsaking it must have taken tortured hours of brooding. And now, at 65, he was forsaking a world he had created and lived with the major part of his life.

The reasons for this abandonment of a cosmos in which he was the chief deity must have been most persuasive. "Li'l Abner" was the magic carpet he once rode in the DeWitt Theatre in New Haven. The comic strip had made him rich and famous. And now he was finished with it.

Had he dried up? Run out of ideas? I don't think so. His imagination had not failed him. Only his energy was ebbing. He was tired. He didn't want to think on a deadline schedule any more. Forty-three years of dreaming up plots and characters had been, for the most part, a joyous voyage of unexpected delights, of fruitful explorations of a mind that poured out its fantastic treasures of the quaint and curious, the droll and the freakish. To be able to live and prosper doing what you wanted to do, to work with exultation, and love what you have fashioned was a life-style Alfred had achieved, and was now abdicating.

"What will you do?" I asked.

"First, go to England. Maybe write. Always wanted to, you know."

My brother never considered himself a truly talented artist. He labored at the drawing board and achieved a style fashioned from his adoration of the great illustrators Phil May and Aubrey Beardsley. His figures were anatomically correct, a tribute to the years spent at a host of art schools drawing from live models. His pen line was strong and clean. His true genius with the pen, however, came from the faces of his characters.

95

Abner, Daisy Mae, Pappy, the scrofulous Scraggs, the miserable citizens of Lower Slobbovia—all were distinct personalities mined from the lodestones of Alfred's prodigious imagination. Each of his faces was a marvelous reflection of what he contrived to say about these people. His good people were luminous, but crafty. His knaves and scoundrels were hideous but understandably so. One never hated his villains; rather you felt an affinity for the most fiendish of Capp's creatures because somehow they reminded you of somebody you knew. Possibly of yourself.

"Li'l Abner" continuities were illustrated stories. Alfred loved writing them. Why not retire from the demanding labors of pencilling, inking, lettering, correcting and simply writing? Why not? And why not in England where my brother had many friends and where he loved the mood and the manners.

Catherine remained in Cambridge while Alfred flew to England to buy a flat. He favored the Belgravia district where he had for years rented an apartment owned by Joshua Logan, the Broadway and Hollywood director.

Normally, weeks or even months could pass without any communication between Alfred and me. For some reason I still don't understand, I began to worry about my brother. He had left for England not in the best of moods, nor in robust health. I phoned Catherine.

"No, I haven't heard from Al," Catherine reported. "And that's odd. Really odd."

"Why odder than his usual silences?" I asked.

"Well, he knew the apartment he wanted. He said he'd phone me as soon as he got the lease or bought the place. But..." Catherine was evidently disturbed, "but he hasn't called. And..."

"You know how to reach him?"

"He always stays at the Savoy."

"Have you phoned him there?"

Catherine hesitated. "Well, you know how he is"

Yes. He hated being "checked on." Phoning him at the Savoy would have been checking. Catherine was loathe to do so.

"Would you?"

Yes, I told her, I would call. It was midnight, London time, when I reached the desk at the Savoy. No, Mr. Capp wasn't there. Yes, he had been there, but last Wednesday he had checked out. Sorry. No forwarding address.

A few minutes after I had hung up the phone in puzzlement, I called the Savoy once again. This time I asked for the night manager. He came on, and for the next two hours this imperturbable and decent man played Sherlock Holmes for me. It was almost three a.m. London time when the night manager filed his final telephonic report.

"Mr. Capp returned to this hotel about midnight last Wednesday. As he was about to enter his suite, he must have fainted. We know that he is not a drinking man, and the night clerk instantly phoned for a doctor.

"Your brother, fully conscious but obviously in some discomfort, disclosed his relationships—"

"What," I broke in. "What relationships? I mean...?"

The night manager tittered. "Sorry about my choice of words, Mr. Caplin...I should have said 'relations,' not 'relationships'."

"What relations?" I must have sounded very stupid.

"Why, Mr. Caplin, your brother informed us he had at least a dozen cousins in London who were doctors. Doctors of medicine, that is."

Of course! A branch of my mother's family escaping from Czarist Russia in the 1800s had come to England via South Africa. The patriarch of the Sacks family (my grandmother's maiden name was Sacks) had apparently inspired his children with his own unrealized dream of becoming a physician in a land where Jews were permitted this liberty to serve, possibly cure and certainly have a better life than the Sacks had led in the ghetto of Riga, Latvia.

And it was true. At least a dozen of the Sacks family had become doctors. Thus, when the untiring night manager of the Savoy had checked the phone book for a "Dr. Sacks," he stumbled upon a treasure trove of medical second cousins to tend the needs of my ailing brother. Ever the diplomat, the night manager phoned all of them! Winston Churchill in his final moments was not better attended than Alfred Caplin was at the London Clinic.

The next morning, Catherine flew to London. The day after, my sister Madeline took off from New York to visit her ailing brother. And one week later, when Alfred was out of danger, I arrived in England.

My brother was back at the Savoy. He seemed subdued rather than defeated. The diagnosis of the various medical relatives suggested Alfred was suffering from exhaustion complicated by emphysema and lupus. It was a combination of these last two that would eventually destroy him.

To be confronted at odd hours of the morning by impeccably accented cousins he had never set eyes on bewildered and then invigorated Alfred. Sensibly, he decided only one doctor would be in charge of his case.

"Sounds simple, eh?" My brother was reviewing his often nightmarish experiences. "I mean, you pick out one doctor and he's in charge. Well, not with our cousins. Hell, these people loathe each other! They discussed my case out in the hospital—I mean clinic—corridor, but at the top of their lungs. Momma would have been proud of their diction!"

Finally, one of the cousins was designated chief of staff of this covey of medical kinfolk and he proved efficient and kindly. And, Alfred avowed, "he looks and talks like Uncle Archie." Archie, you will recall, was my mother's youngest brother who forfeited a dancing career to man the pulpit at an orthodox synagogue in Lebanon, Pa.

A week passed. Each day, I would visit with my brother. We talked. About a play I was working on. About my children. We discussed what life would be like in London. What we never discussed was his feeling that there was very little left for him to do. Even the writing he had planned as a new career now appeared remote and strangely unrewarding. At least that was the impression he gave by his refusal to discuss his own deep feelings.

On my last day in London (Alfred was to fly home the next week) I wheeled him down to the lobby, accompanied by Miss Flint, his nurse. Miss Flint was an attenuated version of Alec Guinness in starched white drag. She was tiny, precise, and given to tragic head shakings on the deplorable conditions in the world today, England especially, and Buckingham Palace most notably.

Miss Flint stood primly between Alfred and me in the deserted card room of the hotel. She refused to sit down, contending she was "on duty." Obviously practical nurses in the British Isles are constrained either by tradition or prejudice from flexing their knees at work.

Alfred turned to me; his shoulders were hunched in anticipation of what he was about to create. I recognized the birthing gesture and prepared to join whatever outrage he was plotting to perpetrate on the resolutely vertical Nurse Flint.

"It's a shame, isn't it!"

"A rotten shame," I concurred.

"You'd think he'd have confessed a long time ago."

"Ages ago," I nodded, containing my own growing curiosity. Miss Flint stiffened noticeably. We had her attention. All of it.

Under her nurse's cap annealed to a rigidity that must have constricted the flow of blood from her heart to brain and vice versa, her pale blue eyes were alert to what she must have prayed was to be a scandalous revelation. Her breath came in wispy gusts; she edged closer to Alfred.

"Imagine." Alfred shook his head seemingly overwhelmed by what he was to imagine.

"Imagine." I knew enough of my brother's creative procedure not to even guess at what he imagined.

"And she never suspected!"

"How could she?" I was in the groove, without having the remotest idea where this groove led.

"And to think they share the same room, the same bed—" Alfred's voice had dipped to a tragic octave.

"Unthinkable!" I exclaimed, hoping he would come to the point because I was getting as antsy as the trembling Miss Flint.

"And," Alfred was struggling with the enormity of what he was about to disclose. "And..."

Nurse Flint was unable to constrain herself. "And?" she whispered reverently.

"And," my brother's voice caught. "And to think it all happened at Buckingham Palace!"

"Buckingham Palace!" Nurse Flint screamed. "What the bloody hell happened at Buckingham Palace?"

Alfred looked at me. "You tell her." He clearly implied he hadn't the heart to say what must be said...about Buckingham Palace, that is.

I remembered that Alfred had always had problems finishing a story in the comic strip. His beginnings and middles were marvels of humor and hilarious explorations of absurd premises; he admitted that he lost interest in the endings to these exploits because they should make sense, and making sense in a conventional manner was not what interested Al Capp.

So, he left the finale up to me. And if I didn't come up with something, Nurse Flint gave every indication that she would explode into tiny white fragments far beyond the most competent surgeon's ability to reunite. It was my duty to end this story and save Miss Flint's endangered life.

"Well," I was desperately waiting for inspiration. "Well..." it came, the inspiration or what I hoped as a reasonable facsimile. "Prince Philip never told the Queen the truth—about himself, that is."

Alfred's attention sharpened. Miss Flint was speechless with tremulous anticipation. "Go on," he prompted. "Tell Miss Flint the whole sordid story."

Sordid it was to be. Or at least sordid by Nurse Flint's standards. "Prince Philip is not only not a prince..."

Nurse Flint gasped and wavered, gripping the back of Alfred's chair for support.

"Not a prince..." You could hardly hear her.

"Not only not a prince," I plowed on, emboldened by Alfred's obvious fascination with my recital, "but the son of an orthodox rabbi!"

Nurse Flint yelped like a cornered fox. "You're saying that Prince Philip is..." She was gagging on her unexpressed thought.

This was no time to beat around the bush. "That's right. Prince Philip is a Hebrew." I had decided to say "Hebrew" instead of "Jew," hoping that word might help de-contaminate the bogus Prince in the eyes of Nurse Flint.

Nurse Flint was beyond niceties. "That means that...that Prince Charles is—Oh, my God!" Nurse Flint sat down while on duty, perhaps for the first time in her career.

"Oh, my God," she repeated, "the Kind of England will be..." She lapsed into what struck me as a comatose condition.

Alfred ordered a brandy for Nurse Flint. She drank it in one quivering gulp, rearranged her cap and stood up. Bravely, I thought.

"If you don't mind, Mr. Capp, I should like to return you to your quarters. My relief is due to arrive momentarily." We returned to Alfred's suite. Nurse Flint left without a word, and, I understand, failed to show up for work the following morning.

One week later my brother flew back to Boston. He did not return to England. Apparently, Nurse Flint never revealed her secret knowledge of Prince Philip's dark past. At least, not to Margaret Thatcher.

Li'l Abner and Al Capp. © Capp Enterprises, Inc. Reprinted with permission.

Li'l Abner and Mammy Yokum. © Capp Enterprises, Inc. Reprinted with permission.

Daisy Mae. Reprinted with permission.

© Capp Enterprises, Inc. Reprinted with permission.

Fearless Fosdick. © Capp Enterprises, Inc. Reprinted with permission.

Li'l Abner, Daisy Mae Scragg, "Honest Abe" Yokum, Mammy Yokum, Pappy Yokum, Salomey and Tiny. Reprinted with permission.

Sadie Hawkins. © Capp Enterprises, Inc. Reprinted with permission.

SALOMEY and PAPPY YOKUM

Above is a panel from "Al Capp by Li'l Abner," done in the 1940s by Capp for servicemen-amputees. © Capp Enterprises, Inc. Reprinted with permission.

Long Distance

The year was 1957. Alfred had been with United Features Syndicate for over 20 acrimonious years. His original contract gave the Syndicate ownership of "Li'l Abner," a possession that my brother abhorred and fought against in increasing acrimony as his comic strip grew in importance.

United Features had grudgingly agreed after two bloody decades to cede Alfred his creation. They had little or no choice. And they were making money from the features.

Now, in 1957, my brother and I were seated in the offices of a prestigious law firm, Poletti and Diamond. Mr. Diamond, Sr. was a man of Buddah-like dimensions and infinite wisdom. He and his son, also a lawyer, listened to Alfred's colorful version of his stormy relationship with his syndicate, nodding in gentle harmony with Alfred's emphatic hand and head motions.

Mr. Diamond's subtle prodding robbed Alfred's version of much of the drama he instinctually embroidered into any story he might tell, and arrived at a lawyer's skeletal structure of a legal matter. Elaboration could come later, Mr. Diamond must have concluded, when he and his client faced a jury of "L'il Abner" fans.

"And so I conclude, Mr. Capp, that now that you own your own feature, you wish to sever relationships with United Features and offer your comic strip to another syndicate?"

"Exactly," Mr. Capp approved.

"I see," Mr. Diamond smiled benignly. "And may I see your contract with United Features?"

"Of course you may," Alfred replied graciously.

Mr. Diamond waited, shifted his bulk, and looked at his son. His son shrugged in a gesture that might have had some significance for the elder Diamond.

"I gather," he spoke soothingly, as though to a Down's syndrome victim, "I gather that you don't have the contract on your person, Mr. Capp?"

"On my person!" Alfred was obviously stunned by the suggestion that

111

he had come to a lawyer's office fully prepared for a litigious experience.

The younger Diamond fully comprehended my brother's bewilderment. He faced his father, now twitching in taciturn concern that somehow he had lost control of the meeting.

"Mr. Capp is from Boston, Dad." He then faced Alfred, smiling apologetically as one does through the bars at the zoo when facing a surly male lion. "Perhaps we could call your office and have them send the contract to us"?

"Great idea," Alfred concurred. He made a gesture toward the phone on the desk.

"Oh, my God!" The younger Diamond groaned.

"Why? I mean, what's the matter?" The elder Diamond had forsaken his lofty reserve. His son's sudden ashy coloration must have brought out the parent in him.

"The strike!" The younger Diamond was crushed.

Of course. There was a telephone operator's strike in the New York area and although local calls were eventually completed, long distance was out of the question.

The elder Diamond had regained his composure. He regarded us with the benevolence of a Father Damien. "I think we'd best have Junior join us."

The younger Diamond beamed, the color returning to his cheeks. "Of course. I'll get him." He arose and left the room. We waited in silence, the elder Diamond never once losing his dreadful concentration on remaining bountiful and at the same time commandingly judicial.

We waited for Junior. No effort was made at small talk. Mr. Diamond continued to beam like the Sandy Hook lighthouse. Alfred tapped his good leg in rhythmic impatience. I wondered who and what Junior was.

The door was flung open and held in place by a reverential young Mr. Diamond. And in strode Junior. Here was a man made indeed for striding. He was well over six feet in height and moved with the grace and authority of a Kabuki war lord.

Junior exuded confidence, featuring a smile of such warmth and dimension that we all felt mulched by its radiance. His tailoring was a tasteful mixture of Ivy League reticence emboldened by a New York City flair for suave conformity.

And yes, there was something hauntingly familiar about Junior. It took only seconds to figure it out. We were in the presence of Franklin Delano Roosevelt, Jr., lawyer and member of this firm. Reaching maturity as we did in the golden age of this man's father, we were impressed as probably we would never be again by any other public or semi-public figure. Here we were in the same room with the flesh and blood of the man we considered to be the greatest human being that ever lived. At least we thought so in 1957.

And his son was shaking hands with us and smiling that iridescent Roosevelt smile!

Other than a few mumbled awed syllables, no words were exchanged until the elder Diamond said, "Franklin, would you mind putting through a long-distance call to Boston for Mr. Capp?"

"Of course!" Franklin beamed and with a graceful swipe gathered the phone in his hand.

"Hello? I wish to place a call to Boston. This is Franklin Delano Roosevelt, Jr." He paused, listening and then nodded his head and smiled.

"Thank you," he said into the phone, "thank you very much." Franklin Delano Roosevelt, Jr. handed the phone to my brother.

"If you'll just give the young lady your number..."

My brother gave the young lady the number. Franklin bowed slightly, waved his hand in a gesture reminiscent of his father on the campaign trail, and exited.

We completed our business and left the law office wondering what duties a Franklin Roosevelt, Jr. performed when there was no telephone strike.

At Bay

To achieve prominence in any field requires talent, the recognition of that talent and a kind of hubris that will mock humility should any concealed weakness surface.

Alfred qualified. He fashioned a public persona that was far more genial than his private person. When he was the sole celebrity in any gathering, he was gracious, witty and pleasantly obliging. Even modest when there was no call for diffidence.

In the company of other celebrities the strain to establish the uniqueness of his position in his own world could give a man a severe headache. Surrounded by stars on the stage and screen, Alfred would hold his own with a minimum of effort. After all, he wrote his own material; his voice was resonant, his laugh infectious. And he created daily and Sunday. He was universal and beloved and had held that position for years and years. Actors and actresses admired him and he reveled in his eminence.

With savants, writers, and experts in specific fields, Alfred was more subdued. He competed for their attention and the applause of the audience carefully judging the cartoonist versus the brain. In the presence of a Kissinger, a Galbraith, and Schlesinger, a Steinbeck or Updike, Alfred fashioned his spoken dialogue with the precision and cunning of a miniaturist.

My brother was admired by John Steinbeck to the point where the writer remarked to me jocularly but with evident admiration, "Al Capp should be awarded the Nobel Prize in literature." When I reported this comment to Alfred he said, "Well, get on it." To this day I don't know how serious he was about my getting in touch with the King of Sweden. Needless to say, I didn't. And to this day, I wonder what would have happened if I had.

How important his fame was to him I could never judge. Beyond a doubt, he enjoyed being recognized. But he never allowed his prominence to taint his family relationships. He never posed or boasted; his generosity to relatives he hardly knew became our family's legend. Momma, on her death bed, implored her eldest son to take care of one of her brothers who hadn't quite made it as a businessman, but had scored frequently as a

115

husband and father.

Alfred put two of Momma's indigent brother's sons through college. As far as I know, he never met either of these boys, now successful professional men. A favorite aunt was ill for the last 20 years of her life. Alfred paid all her medical bills promptly. My brother's generosity was extensive and cheerfully given. There was only one requirement: the recipient of the gift had to be truly in need.

In the last years of his life, Alfred ailed. His constant smoking caused emphysema. Odd and often exotic eating habits wrecked his digestive system. He also developed a form of lupus. And the artificial leg got heavier and heavier. Walking even the shortest distances became an agony.

What damaged his self-esteem and wounded him most deeply, however, was what he considered to be an egregious defection by his friends because of his gradually deepening criticism of what he chose to call "liberal frauds." His attacks on public figures whose judgment and honesty he questioned made enemies not only of his targets, but of men and women who decided that Al Capp had become a hardened right-wing reactionary.

For the whole of his professional life, Alfred had reveled in taking aim at targets he loathed for their perfidy and hypocrisy. In "L'il Abner," he splayed victims with such lustful revulsion there was no room for compassion, only gleeful endorsement of Al Capp's decapitation of his prey.

Captains of industry, politicians, poseurs, super salesmen of worthless chattels, intellectual frauds, cheats, fools and con artists were all scourged by Alfred. He ridiculed, satirized relentlessly the fakery he found rampant in public and private life. No one was spared in the crematorium of Al Capp's comic strip panels, daily and Sunday.

Margaret Mitchell (via her lawyers) threatened Alfred with a law suit that would have resulted in his paying damages roughly equivalent to the cost of building the Panama Canal. "Li'l Abner" had parodied Miss Mitchell's sensational book *Gone With the Wind* with a pitiless attack on the more specious and mawkish sentiments of Rhett, Scarlett, Melanie et al.

Normally contentious when challenged, Alfred decided to apologize in print. He devised a continuity in which he acknowledged the Mitchell claims of scurrility, and proceeded to explain with mock servility why he was sorrowful for what he had done to Rhett, Scarlett, Melanie et al.

Showing good common sense and a sharpened judgment in anticipating public reaction to Capp's apology, the Mitchell team hastened to assure the cartoonist that they would accept this atonement without his bothering to print a comic page expiation.

The popular singer Joan Baez inevitably came under Alfred's scrutiny. Miss Baez, possessor of a lovely and haunting voice, had become the deserving darling of what used to be called "the Masses." This composite of the defiant, the unemployed, the dissatisfied, the rebellious—almost all young people—thronged to Miss Baez's concerts, bought her recordings by the tens of thousands and made her quite prosperous.

Capp dipped his pen in a withering mixture of venom and irony and came up with "Joanie Phoney," an idolized singer of songs of protest. He relentlessly parodied Joanie's public displays of selfless devotion to lost causes and dedication to the needs of the poor and deprived while tooling around in a chauffeur-driven limo of immense proportions. By her own admission (in a recently published biography) Miss Baez admitted that Capp had had a point. This in no way diminished her hatred for the cartoonist, but she showed her innate honesty and frank evaluation of herself in acknowledging that her lifestyle and her public avowals showed some discrepancies.

So when Alfred, in later years, shifted his range of attack from the stuffed icons of the right to what he considered to be the fakes, the deceivers, the malingerers of the liberal left, he did so with a firm conviction that he hadn't changed, "they had."

At first with amiable intent, Alfred ridiculed the sometimes strident friend and defender of minorities, Senator Ted Kennedy. He was relentless in his mockery of able-bodied collectors of welfare funds. And he assaulted with grim relish young people who he claimed stole hub caps, practiced public puberty, sneered at convention, rarely if ever bathed and in general offended all his treasured instincts.

There was no concentrated effort to force Alfred to change his attitude. The besiegement just grew until it began to infect his public disposition; his frequent appearances as guest speaker on college campuses became embattled skirmishes between Capp and the students. Properly reared young men and women launched savage and often profane grenades at the speaker. He was accused of a litany of offenses to liberal causes that were no more bizarre than they were unfounded.

After a few sobering exposures to these assaults, Alfred found himself actually enjoying the savage give-and-take of the face-offs. On one occasion, when a planned exodus from the auditorium threatened to sabotage his address, Alfred departed from the prepared text. He held up his hand to signal a change in sequence.

"I see several of you people leaving here, two by two. I want you to know that I fully understand your haste in getting the hell out of this hall, and I want to assure you that I've been told by the committee in charge of the medical mobile unit parked outside that they'll wait for any and all of you who want to be tested for the possibility that you've contracted a venereal disease. So, take your time, boys and girls. They've got a lot of needles to spare."

It was not Capp at his best, but it worked. The students actually gave him a standing ovation. Some were even mildly surprised that there was no mobile unit parked outside.

More serious than the animosity of college students was the splenetic reaction of some members of the press at Al Capp's political "turnabout." Jack Anderson, the columnist who had inherited the syndicated feature "Washington Merry Go-Round," founded by two truly able journalists, Drew Pearson and Robert Allen, prospered when he unearthed any evidence to bash politicians—or anybody of note—if and when dalliance was discovered.

Anderson was widely read. For the most part, he was reasonably accurate in his versions of events, most of them of a political nature. He had no known personal animosity against Al Capp. Nor any known affection. He and his staff were fully aware that a columnist cannot exist writing only about happenings already reported in the newspaper.

Newspapers and press services chose to ignore a story coming out of a southern university town that Capp had been accused of an indiscretion with a local coed. Jack Anderson decided it was worth a column. He assigned, as he often did, one of his minor accomplices, Brit Hume, to do the piece. Hume had no impressive qualifications either as a writer or investigator. However he did the story and its publication caused, understandably, embarrassment and pain for Alfred and his family.

The marvelous creative energies that had fueled my brother throughout most of his life began to ebb. He fought his truculent critics with ever-diminishing vigor. His old friends, many of them noted Harvard teachers, shunned Al Capp as though he were a contagious malignancy. "Hell hath no fury," Alfred once commented, "like a Liberal scorned."

As his health failed, Alfred stopped going on the lecture circuit. He spent more and more time in London, a city that knew him not as a cartoonist, but as a witty commentator who appeared frequently on their television and who wrote a bright, funny column for the "Spectator."

The death of his daughter, Cathy, and the brutal murder of his eldest granddaughter by a drunken driver seemed to shrivel Alfred. He became moody and silent; he seemed to know he was failing. He died quietly as he reached his 70th birthday and was buried in a country cemetery outside Amesbury, Massachusetts. A minister and a rabbi officiated at the grave.

Autobiography

Psychiatrists invent labels for the misfortunes that frequently infest our lives, as though giving a name or title to an ugly and demeaning experience automatically endows it with stature.

When Alfred became famous as a maverick humorist both in his comic strips and as a frequent guest on popular talk shows, the label-givers, the between-the-liners exulted.

"He's compensating for the amputation of his leg by demonstrating to the world that he's more than made up for the loss of a limb by thumbing his nose at the world." This was one magazine writer's explanation for my brother's consistent brushes with convention, his contempt for the establishment.

When I showed Alfred the magazine piece, he reacted calmly. I expected him to rage. Instead he cooly stated his rebuttal.

"Maybe the guy's right. But if he is, I'm surprised. I never think in terms of a limb loss. Sitting down, drawing my pictures or writing some copy, I work with my head. Not with my ankle, kneecap or my thighs. No inspiration there. Sitting down, the legs don't matter. The hands, yes. I write with them. The brain, of course. That's where it all comes from. No, I don't agree with the man."

There were probably several data-based conclusions one could reach to explain many of Al Capp's attitudes, biases, hang-ups. He had drawn his own. "No," he once explained to me. "No, I'm not at all interested in what makes me the person I am. I cheerfully accept the inspirations that wind up, often enough, as good comic strip material. Where they come from I haven't the foggiest notion. Nor does anybody else know. You'd have to dredge up a billion years of genealogical history to explain who I am and what I do. Why bother excavating? Not I, certainly."

Compiling a psychological profile on Alfred would be an awesome assignment. The psychobiographers who dredge through the banana peels of their subject's life often confuse the garbage for the genuine character of their subject.

In Alfred's case, a dedicated biographer would be obliged to study and analyze the writings and drawings to find some clue to his personality traits

121

or his social facade. That dictates a studious perusal of well over 100,000 drawings that Al Capp produced in his lifetime.

And the biographer would have to immerse himself in multitudes of plots that varied from raucous criticisms of status quo to idyllic liaisons between boy and girl. The only consistency in Al Capp's prodigious output was the often acrid smell of disappointment in man and his callous contempt for his co-existers on earth.

When Alfred decided to end his cartooning career in 1977, it signaled to several publishers a retirement that might lead to an autobiography. The assumption was that should Al Capp agree to a revelation of his life's experience, the result would be sensational.

Since my brother had no apparent interest in reviewing a life he now seemed weary of, the publishers turned to me. The first call was from the head of one of the leading paperback companies.

"We know your brother has led a colorful life. We think there's a vast public out there who want to know more about..." The publisher hesitated. "...about his...brushes with convention. Al Capp was himself a writer, so what is written, he writes. Think he'll be interested?" And the publisher mentioned an impressive advance payment, a "ball park figure."

I phoned Alfred and repeated my conversation. After a contemplative silence, he spoke. "You know, I've thought about it, but hell, I don't think I want to. Look if you can get a good writer to work with me, maybe I'd do it."

"Have you anybody in mind?" I asked.

"Yes, Jimmy Breslin." I was somewhat surprised. Breslin was a talented observer of contemporary events. He was sharply observant and very humorous. But I never associated him or his style with my brother.

Alfred went on. "Surprised, huh? Well, don't be. I like him. We went on a trip together to Japan for some government project after the end of the war. I learned to respect Breslin. And he's a damn good writer."

Jimmy Breslin was flattered, he said, but too busy with his own work to take on a biography of another man.

So started a series of conversations with authors which uncovered enmities I scarcely knew existed and exposed some celebrated writers as often mean-spirited greedy word-merchants.

One said to me, "Sure, I'll work with the son of a bitch. But the advance stays in my pocket. Your brother can have the glory. I want the cash."

Another assured me, "Capp and I are at the opposite ends of the political poles. If he accepts my prejudices, I'll tolerate his. Is it a deal?" It was not.

As I reported these interviews to my brother, his enthusiasms for collaboration waned until he sighed and told me, "Forget it. I may take a shot at it myself."

Three months later my wife and I were in Cambridge to visit our children. I phoned Alfred. He seemed somewhat subdued as he asked me to drop in and said that he would like to "show me something."

The attitude was puzzling. He had never asked me to drop in before. In our life no family member or close friend "dropped in." He came unannounced, famished, and utterly confident he'd be welcomed and fed.

The house on Brattle Street looked as serene as ever. The white picket fence had been newly painted and reflected the spurious quality of the New England character.

These thoughts had taken over as I entered my brother's house. I knew, as I always knew, that I would feel that both he and I were guests in this alien land.

We greeted each other with the casual pleasantness that was our style, irrespective of the amount of time that had passed between visits, or emotional cataclysm that had recently betrayed our tranquillity.

He was seated in his wheel chair. For the past several months he had been unable to walk more than a step or two. The house had been fitted with chair lifts so that Alfred had been able to descend to the lower floor when he wished.

"I did it, God help me," he announced smiling sheepishly.

"You did—what?" It was then I noticed the sheaf of yellow papers wedged close to his side.

Alfred pulled out the sheaf and handed it to me. "The biography I said I wouldn't do. It's not finished. But..." he appeared strangely self-conscious. "Well, hell, take a look at it and tell me what you think."

We chatted for a few minutes. My brother seemed uncomfortable, not at all like the relaxed person he had always been with me. I rose to leave.

"When," he hesitated, "when do you think you'll read it?"

"Tonight," I replied. "We're seeing the kids for dinner, and when they're gone, I'll get to it." I hefted the manuscript. "There are only about...what ? Sixty or seventy pages?

"Seventy-four," Alfred said. He squirmed in his chair. It was clear he didn't want to discuss it until I'd read what he had written.

I left and returned to the hotel.

That night, after the children had gone, I started to read my brother's manuscript. My wife was watching me, I knew. I tried to keep my expressions bland. Why? I think because I began to feel that I must lie about what a premonition warned me was to be a harrowing experience.

It was. Was a harrowing experience.

Not that the story didn't abound with charming anecdotes. There were a few beguiling takes of Al Capp's youth; there appeared warmly affectionate experiences with friends and relatives. It was as though Alfred was raised a Bobbsey Twin and led a life bereft of stress and tension. Nowhere in the 70-odd pages did I find the man I knew. Only a pale caricature of a candy cane creature, as though a child had asked his father to tell him about his childhood, and the parent had responded with sanitized versions of his existence in order to give his kid a rainbow and a simple road map to the pot of gold.

My wife knew before I spoke a word. "Bad?" she asked me.

"No, bad isn't the word. More...unreal...concealing... defensive..."

Silence for many minutes. My wife spoke. "What are you going to tell him?"

I didn't know. "I'll think about it."

I thought about it most of a sleepless night. About dawn I made up my mind.

I'd lie.

The phone rang at eight. It was Alfred.

"Well, did you manage to wade through the stuff?"

"I'll be at your house in about an hour. We'll talk then. O.K.?"

"Sure. Don't rush, take your time." He was imploring me to come quickly. I began to feel ill.

"Are you sure you're doing the right thing?" My wife was as taut and anxious as I was.

"It's all I can think to do," I replied.

"But lying—" She was manifestly uncomfortable with my decision.

"What else can I do? Tell him the truth? Tell him the stuff is awful? What good will that do?"

No good at all. And besides, maybe my judgment was lopsided. I was not a literary critic. Could be that Alfred's taciturn concealment of the truth was what the book-buying public wanted and expected from the creator of the beloved Li'l Abner and the Dogpatch critters.

But I didn't believe a word of my self-assurance. And I was about to enter the front door of 124 Brattle Street and confront my terminally ill brother. He waited for me, seated in his wheel chair. He was carefully groomed as though preparing for a job interview with an unpredictable employer. The smile he greeted me with had more of grimness in it than cheery welcome.

"Well, tell me the worst." He was struggling to keep the discussion on a plane of no consequence. As if it didn't bother him and what else is new. It was no use. He was suffering.

"I loved the way you handled the art director's job at Transogram Toys," I began. Buffeted by my own deceptions, with the wind at my back, I sailed the treacherous channels of my perjuries beatified by the personal sacrifice of treasured principles. Alfred listened to me, nodding occasionally. The emphasis I put on the scattered memorabilia that now and again held attention gave me sufficient basis for enthusiasm. And I milked every one of the infrequent readable scenes with seeming relish.

Throughout this performance, Alfred never took his eyes from me. His body was hunched forward, his hands clenched by his side. When I finished my enthusiastic review, he smiled and thanked me. We chatted for a few minutes, and I left the house, exhausted but satisfied that I had given my brother some reason to feel pleased and fulfilled.

How wrong I was.

I had forgotten something.

It was when I returned to New York that same evening and got a phone call from my sister Madeline that I remembered what I had forgotten.

"What did you do to Alfred?" my sister demanded of me.

"Do? What do you mean—what did I do to Alfred? I read his manuscript and told him..."

"Told him you hated it!" Madeline was indignant.

"Hated it! Hated it! I told Alfred it was great! I told him how much I enjoyed...enjoyed a whole lot of it! What do you mean 'I hated it'?"

Madeline was calmer now. "Well, he phoned me after you left his house and told me you'd been there. That you had read some of his autobiography and that, well, he said that the strain of finding something nice to say about his writing aged you right in front of his eyes. He treated it like a joke...only..." She didn't have to continue. I knew.

I knew that neither I nor anybody else who came in contact with Alfred could ever deceive him. Whether it was instinct, talent, or an extraordinary perceptual sense, I don't know. My brother had this uncanny ability to sweep away conceits masquerading as openness; he was always able to penetrate the cunning ambushes people structured to mask their true selves.

And my less than stunning performance as a counterfeit critic hadn't fooled him for a minute.

He never wrote another word of his autobiography.

Cohen's Egg Farm

It was one of those hot July days when the brain was baked into insensitivity and the body operated robotically solely to ensure continuity of existence. Conversation was held to a minimum as my wife and I drove along the Connecticut shore on our way to visit our daughters simmering in a camp in Rhode Island.

The top of our convertible was down against my wife's admonition that we would soon be broiled into carbonized calcium before we reached the girls' cabins. But I was stubbornly determined to achieve a tanned body even though at my age interest in my pigmentation by others than myself was limited or nonexistent.

We idled along the Connecticut superhighway. The road had little attraction for us. It was one of those endless concrete ribbons designed by pragmatic men for efficient travel, not for whimsical rumination—the kind that made driving side roads so alluring.

Bored and thirsty, I turned off the highway and began a search for some rural oasis that, I reasoned, had to be lurking somewhere near the narrow rutted country road we now traveled.

Trees arched over us. There was no traffic and suddenly I heard this internal buzzing. It was an alarm going off in my brain. I struggled to give meaning to this abrupt spasm of undefined thought, and failed. It was like waiting for a traffic light to change from red to amber.

My wife was studying me with some concern.

"Something wrong?" she inquired.

"I don't know," I answered. "But this place...I mean this road...the trees...something about the—" I hesitated, reluctant to provide proof that indeed my brain was being neutered by the heat.

"Go on. Something about the—the what?" my wife persisted.

"I..." It was going to sound insane. "I think I've been here before."

"Here on a county road outside of... Where are we outside of, anyway?"

"I think..." and then it came to me in a rush of memories. "I think we're about 20 miles from New Haven."

"You were born there, weren't you?" my wife inquired.

Yes, I was born in New Haven. In 1918 three of the four Caplin children came down with mumps. Only Alfred escaped. Convinced that the only cure lay in inhaling huge gobs of "fresh country air," Momma searched for an uncovered accommodation for herself and her three convalescents in a *kochelane* outside of the village of Branford, Connecticut. Alfred remained in New Haven with my father.

A *kochelane* was no more nor less than a boarding house with trees, chickens, perhaps a cow or two, and the clean country air Momma was dead set on siphoning into her children's lungs. We—all four of us—shared one room. The kitchen was communal, with time set aside for each family's cooking needs.

Cohen's Egg Farm was owned by Abe and Rose Cohen, displaced farmers from Latvia. Wisely, the Cohens were rarely visible. All contacts with boarders were left in the hands of Dovidal (David), the 17-year-old son of Abe and Rose. I recall Dovidal vividly as a tall (I was five at the time) smiling young man with a mass of curly black hair, the reddest cheeks I had ever seen, and a marvelous set of glistening white teeth. We children worshipped "Big Dovidal" and he seemed to enjoy our adulation.

It was while we were rusticating and breathing deeply at Cohen's that Alfred suffered his accident. And the late afternoon telephone call from my father to my mother I can recall with horrifying detail.

The telephone had been newly installed by Abe Cohen, and next to his chickens was his proudest possession. It rarely rang, to be sure, since very few of the Cohen's friends or relatives had bothered to invest in this luxury. And certainly few of the boarders could afford a telephone or had any desire to subscribe to a manifestly superfluous service.

The phone rang and all within earshot of this rare event rushed to the kitchen where the device had been installed on the wall. Dovidal answered, and the rest of us clustered around waiting to find out who? or what? or why?

Dovidal listened, nodding his head. Without a word, he faced his audience. He handed the phone to my mother. Momma froze. A phone call was like a wartime telegram. Only bad news was telegraphed. Only disaster was phoned.

Momma listened. She stood on her tiptoes because for some mysterious reason Mr. Cohen had directed the phone company worker to install the instrument high on the pine board wall. Her expression never altered. Her face had lost all color, but her hand remained steady throughout what must have been a nightmare.

Momma finally spoke. "Does Alfred have blood poisoning?"

What Momma meant was, "Will Alfred survive?"

She listened for a few seconds more, and then hung up the phone. The kitchen was crowded with silent people, looking at my mother with compassion. Momma ignored them. She faced her three children.

"We're going home tonight as soon as Poppa gets here."

None of us asked questions. We knew some dreadful accident had hurt Alfred. Momma remained silent, packing her clothes, the cooking utensils, and the groceries she had brought with her to Cohen's farm. We children put our few belongings into a paper carton and sat on the porch stoop, waiting for our father to arrive.

Poppa drove up in his Model T Ford at sundown. Momma hardly spoke to him. She nodded goodbye to the Cohens and our fellow boarders who stood clustered on the porch watching and whispering to each other. I looked for Dovidal and saw him standing next to his parents. He nodded and waved a discreet goodbye as though afraid to show any emotion in the face of Momma's grimness.

It was dark when we turned from the clearing leading up to the farmhouse and set out on the dirt road which would join a paved highway leading to New Haven.

The children huddled in the back seat. Our parents sat in front. No one spoke. The weak headlights of the old car flickered. There was something wrong with them, but my father never bothered with mechanical details. He would drive this Model T until it stopped dead and he would then dicker for another used car to make his business trip.

I remember the wraiths and apparitions that scurried in between the leaves as the faulty headlights flickered feebly across the branches. I saw ghosts and goblins in the trees and closed my eyes and thought of Dovidal and how he would hand me a peeled orange to eat, or a fresh egg to take to my mother.

Momma broke the silence. "What doctor?'

My father said, "Dr. Blakslee."

Momma: "Why not Dr. Verdi?"

Poppa: "He's not here. Not in New Haven."

Momma: "Where is he?" (Her voice began to rise.)

Poppa: "I don't know."

Momma: "You don't know! You don't know! Then find him. We must have Dr. Verdi!"

Momma's appeal was to God. It was unthinkable to call in a gentile doctor unless he was Verdi. Verdi was a name invoked rather than spoken. Only when life was at stake was Verdi summoned. After Verdi, there was no alternative except Kaddish.

"I'll try to get him," my father replied. His voice trembled.

"You get him, Otto." Momma meant it. Poppa knew it.

Poppa got Dr. Verdi. He was sailing on Long Island Sound when the Coast Guard intercepted him. The surgeon returned to New Haven Hospital the next day, operated and removed Alfred's leg, leaving a stump ten inches in length.

Momma lived in the hospital, sleeping on a cot placed in the corner of Alfred's room. My father and the three children stayed with our *Bubba* Caplin, all sleeping in the attic of the house at 53 Sylvan Avenue.

When we were finally permitted to visit Alfred, I saw Momma for the first time in many weeks. I noticed that she was paler than I had remembered and that her hair had turned white. Alfred seemed smaller and thinner. But otherwise unchanged, at least to his five-year-old younger brother.

"Want to see something?" He was talking to me.

"Sure," I answered. Alfred was always surprising and confusing me with his questions and movements. But he was kind. He never struck me or ridiculed me.

Reaching behind him, Alfred grasped and held up two crutches.

"Watch," he directed me.

He pulled the covers off and we saw the stump, swathed in bandages. Legs—whole legs—were things we all had, were born with. Like a face or hands or a mother and a father, legs were part of you. One didn't spend much time thinking about legs.

But there was only this white lump where a leg should be. I remember thinking...where is it? Where did it go? What happened to legs that were no longer part of someone's body. I felt like vomiting.

Alfred didn't notice. He carefully mounted the crutches and cautiously executed a circle of the room. I edged out as my brother sat on the side of his bed, breathing heavily from the exertion.

I threw up in the corridor and stood panting and guilty as a nurse scolded me. Momma appeared suddenly and took me in her arms, stroking my flushed face.

And now I was back, I thought, where it all began. Almost a half century later I was driving along a country road in Connecticut groping for something to hold on to, to effect a continuity.

"What the hell do you expect?" I hadn't meant to speak out loud. But I had. My wife must have sensed this and remained silent.

What possible difference would it make if this was the rural road that actually led to Cohen's Farm? I would find no messiah there, no fragment from my past that commemorated—what? the tragedy that colored my life and the lives of my brothers, my sister and my parents?

If it were Cohen's farm, Abe and Rose must be dead. And Dovidal? What of Dovidal? I was five when he waved goodbye to me from the stoop. And I never saw him again. Why was I so tense then at the prospect of discovering a new world that was in fact an old world of unspeakable sorrow?

But I had to know.

And then we saw the weatherbeaten, hardly visible sign in front of a sagging house about 100 feet off the road and sitting on a slight incline. The sign read "Cohen's Farm." And underneath in smaller letters hardly discernible it said, "Fresh Eggs for Sale."

The place was unrecognizable. At five it had seemed a vast savannah of trees, plants, flowers woven into a fabric of utter contentment for a small boy who loved the sounds of the country. Dovidal was part of this happiness, the monitor of our pleasures, the guide to the shaded little stream where we waded and the sentinel who stood guard over the odorous but immensely cheerful-sounding hens.

That was when I was five years old. Now it was a scarred and barren land. The stubs of trees were protruding painfully from the earth around the farm house. There were no flowers, and the cackling sound from the hen houses which still stood where I remembered them to be were oddly mournful.

I approached the rear of the farm house, hesitating as I was about to knock on the partially opened door. My wife had said as I exited the car, "You'll probably scare whoever's in that house half to death. Look at you!"

She was right. I was dressed in ragged shorts, no top. My body had been burned an unfashionable red and my hair was in a tangled wind-swept tumulus of black and gray.

"What the hell, they've probably seen worse," I reassured my wife and knocked on the kitchen door.

"Come in," a woman called.

I entered a surprisingly cool room. Two whirling fans criss-crossed the room with bisecting blasts of air. Looking refrigerated in the intersection stood a short lady with an unmistakably grandmotherly attitude. She studied me with a detached curiosity and waited for me to speak. She had been peeling apples over the kitchen counter.

"Is Dovidal here? I mean—" The absurdity of the question was apparent to me, but I seemed helpless to do what I had to do any other way than this.

The short grandmotherly lady was not at all disconcerted by my question, but I did notice she firmed her grip on the knife and angled it generally in my direction.

"My husband's name is David." Her voice was modulated, but her study of me behind her glasses sharpened noticeably.

Encouraged, I burst out, "Does he have black curly hair...and red cheeks...and white teeth? Very white teeth?"

The lady must have decided that although insane, I was harmless. She put her paring knife down on the counter and studied me with what I thought was an expression of compassion, possibly laced with amusement, as though I reminded her of a joke she'd heard a long time ago.

"Black curly hair...red cheeks...white...white teeth..." The lady spoke softly, reminiscently, and her face softened. Maybe, who knows...maybe.

She walked to the rear door, opened it an called toward the hen house, "David! David! You've got company."

Mix exhilaration with an equal part of apprehension and what are you left with? I know. Panic.

What was I doing here in a wind-blown kitchen in a ramshackle farm house waiting for a wraith to rise from a past I'd spent a half-century trying to forget?

Alfred was healthy, rich, famous and as satisfied as he could be. Momma was gone but before she died she had reveled in Alfred's success and all her children were still around and had shucked off the sad past and the melancholy of the "accident." So what in the name of forgetfulness had brought me to the brink of this painful confrontation with a mournful past?

The door of the hen house creaked open and a man stepped out into the littered enclosure adjacent to the coop. He was short and slightly stooped. On his head, wedged down almost concealing his ears, was a battered fedora, stained and creased. It seemed a growth more than an article of apparel.

How could this stunted shambling creature have once been a giant? No way. Dovidal might have shrunk an inch or two. After all, he would have been in his late 70s—if he were alive. But never could Dovidal have been transmogrified into this grotesque caricature. Never.

The woman was speaking. "This gentleman wants to know if Dovidal is here. Are you here, Dovidal?"

The man studied me with the same gentle acceptance of my bizarre appearance as the woman's. "Once, a long time ago, I was called Dovidal." He came closer, peering up into my face. "But how could you know that? I have never seen you before—have I?"

Could it be? Might this really be my Dovidal after all? His cheeks were without color, but what man in his late 70s—other than Santa Claus—has red cheeks? And I could see his teeth. Not the glistening white of a fresh snow drift, but a dingy yellow color like a dimming light bulb of low wattage.

"Would you mind very much removing your hat?" I wondered if it came off, so laminated to his skull was that battle-worn scarred fedora. The man glanced at his wife. She must have nodded assent, because without taking his eyes off me, he pried the old hat off his head.

There wasn't much hair there, and what remained was white. But there were some tufts left still resolutely durable and their texture was sturdy and, yes, curly. And once might have been black.

This was Dovidal. Dovidal 50 years after we had driven off in my father's Model T. Dovidal, indeed.

I was crying. Dovidal seemed to understand. He said, "Who are you, please?"

I told him. He listened and nodded his head. "I remember the lady who got a phone call that told her that her son was hurt bad in an accident. Many times I have wondered what became of the injured boy and the other children who stayed here when my parents rented out rooms to people."

But Dovidal had no memory of the five-year-old worshipper I'd been. Just as well, I decided, as my wife and I drove toward summer camp and reunion with my daughters.

Bennett Harper

One masters the ground rules of suburban living in a panicky scramble. It's a matter of post-haste or perish. You learn to live by the New Haven Railroad's inexorable red and white timetable. Under "Larchmont to New York," the "Leave" column confronts the commuter with an unspeakable lack of alternatives. You "leave Larchmont" at 8:17 or 8:33 (both expresses). You board one of these—or you phone in sick. At least it was that way when I was an editor for a group of magazines that specialized in sagacious advice for parents and obdurate schedules for employees.

My children were aged four, one and newly born when we moved from Brooklyn to the gracious roomy house in Larchmont, N.Y. We fell instantly in love with this quasi-rural living. The only fly in the ointment was the unyielding New Haven R.R. schedule. Oh, well, I reasoned gulping down scalding coffee, you take the bitter with the better.

And then I met the stranger, and life changed for me. He stood at the entrance of the road leading to the garage in the rear of the house. As I backed out with what had become characteristic haste, the stranger remained stationed too close to the driveway, I thought, observing him through the rear view mirror.

I pulled up next to the man. He nodded unsmilingly. I nodded back.

"Need a lift to the station?" It was obvious we had met somewhere and he felt free to cadge a ride.

Without a word, the stranger climbed into the car.

"We met at the...the..." I groped for a name of one of my new neighbors who had given us a "Welcome to Monroe Avenue" party.

He didn't answer. I wondered if he had heard me. We drove a few blocks in an uncomfortable silence. I racked my brain trying to find a clue to this uncommunicative passenger's identity.

"I know who you are." He had finally spoken. "My name is Bennett Harper."

Before I had a chance to answer, he went on, tonelessly, not looking at me but straight ahead.

"You're Al Capp's brother."

"Why yes, I am." The stranger hadn't made his observation in a

135

celebratory tone. He obviously wasn't congratulating me on my relationship to a well-known cartoonist. Although he clearly indicated he needed no verification, I decided to do just that. Mostly because I couldn't think of anything else to say.

More silence as we drove. When we were five blocks from the Railroad Station, my passenger switched his gaze from the windshield to me.

"Don't you see the resemblance?"

Resemblance? To whom? I glanced at Bennett Harper. Straight rather abbreviated nose, sandy hair, thick-lensed glasses, pock marked skin. Nothing memorable about his face. Certainly no "resemblance" to anybody I knew. I shook my head. "No."

"Li'l Abner," Harper said.

I thought I might have missed something. "What about 'Li'l Abner'?" I queried.

Now my passenger was studying me intently. "I resemble 'Li'l Abner.' So much so, I have had to wear smoked glasses so people won't recognize me."

I swerved the car into the curb. Instinct, dormant these many years of reasonably paced living, sprung to life. It alerted me to the fact that a man needed both hands when a nameless feeling of endangerment took charge.

We were more than three blocks from the Railroad parking area.

"Let's walk the rest of the way," I suggested, trying to sound outdoorsy.

The passenger didn't move. "Life has become a living hell for me," he said. "People—even friends—constantly ride me. And you know why, don't you?"

No, I didn't know why. What I did know was that I had to get out of a confined space where I suddenly felt my health was in jeopardy.

Bennett Harper climbed out of the car. His movements were slow and deliberate. "These people keep saying to me, 'Abner, why haven't you had sexual relations with Daisy Mae in the months of August and September!' "

What was most alarming about this encounter was the deadly seriousness of the man's statements. What should have been funny because it was so absurd wasn't funny at all. One look at the stern slightly pained expression on his face demanded that he be taken seriously—or else!

I was frightened. He was a large person, at least two inches taller and about 30 pounds heavier than I. We walked toward the station.

"We'd better hurry if we want to catch this train." I tried to keep my voice level.

"I'm not taking this train. I live in Rye." He had stopped walking and was studying me with his eyes magnified menacingly behind those thick lenses.

"Oh. Your day off?" I was aware that my effort to learn as much about Harper as possible was clumsy, and hoped it wasn't too obvious.

He replied, his voice low, and, I thought, threatening. "Not my day off. Ethyl fired me. And I told you why."

At this point I had no way of knowing that Ethyl wasn't a woman. Ethel was Ethyl, the gasoline additive.

He went on, droningly. "They found out that I was Li'l Abner. That's why I'm not working."

Ethel had to be...it came to me. "You're talking about the Ethyl Gasoline people?"

Harper was walking away. He didn't answer.

I didn't know where he was going. But he was soon out of sight. That mattered. I went into the corner drug store to call and alert my wife. No, that wouldn't work. There was nothing she could do. I phoned the police.

Chief Keresey listened to me. He didn't scoff at what must have sounded like an hysterical account by a worried husband and father of an encounter with a loony bin case.

"Don't worry, Mr. Caplin," he assured me. "I'll have some of my people watch your house. At least until you get home from work. And we won't alarm your wife, if you're worried about that."

Somewhat reassured, I went to my office. Ignoring my calendar, I phoned "Information" and discovered that a Bennett Harper lived on Shady Lane, Rye, New York. I dialed the number and unmistakably Bennett Harper answered the phone. I knew that voice! I hung up. Well, at least he wasn't close to my house and my family. I went to work, but cut the day short by an hour and trained home. And waited.

And waited. A week passed. Still no sign of Bennett Harper. I had decided not to tell my wife of the incident. Chief Keresey proved discreet.

"I see no reason to disturb Mrs. Caplin," he advised me. "There's a good chance this fellow is some kind of nuisance, and you'll never see hide nor hair of him again."

Eight days after the first encounter, on a Sunday at about 2:30, Bennett Harper surfaced. I happened to be looking out the living room window which faced the street (I did a lot of looking out windows since Harper had made his first appearance). I saw him. He was about to enter the path leading to the house.

"Call Chief Keresey and tell him that man is here. He'll know what you're talking about." This was whispered to my wife as I hurried toward the front door. With only a brief questioning glance, she headed for the phone. I was half way down the front path to intercept Bennett Harper when I heard my wife repeat the message to the Larchmont Police Chief.

Harper seemed to have grown in height, weight, and menace since the day he had headed home for Shady Lane, Rye. His eyes were the same, however. They looked dull and lusterless behind those thick lenses.

"It's getting worse," he announced as I grasped his arm and steered him toward the street, away from my wife and children.

"How so?" I said, piloting him toward the beach area, about five blocks from the house.

He sighed, shaking his head sorrowfully.

"Ethyl won't rehire me. Won't even consider it."

A car passed us. It was a noncommital sedan. I recognized the driver. He was Detective Sergeant Crowley of the Larchmont Police force. His eyes were fixed straight ahead. But I knew he saw us, and I felt immensely relieved. Chief Keresey was a man to be reckoned with.

"Exactly what kind of work do you do for Ethyl?" The more I knew about this man, the better equipped I would be to handle any emergency that might come up. At least I hoped so.

"I'm a chemical engineer. Graduated M.I.T. in '47. I've worked for Ethyl ever since. Never had another job but this one. And now—" He stopped walking and faced me. the utter calmness of his voice was terrifying. "And now only two professions are left for me to make a living in."

"And they are?" I couldn't help myself. I had to know.

Bennett Harper had halted and was facing me. Detective Sergeant Crowley passed close by on his return trip. This time he glanced in our direction, slowing his pace moderately.

"Guess," said Harper.

I couldn't. And said so.

"Welding and ski instruction," he said.

"Welding and—" I floundered, groping for a reason.

"Ski instructing." He reached into his pocket and extracted a pair of smoked glasses. Carefully he removed his thick lensed ones and with precise movements donned smoked glasses.

"Now you understand, don't you, Mr. Capp?" I didn't understand and I wished he'd stop calling me Capp. My name was Caplin.

If Harper was irritated with my incomprehension he didn't show it. Without changing the tone of his voice he continued. "Welding and ski instruction are the only two professions where you are expected to wear smoked glasses. When I wear smoked glasses, people won't recognized me as Li'l Abner. So chances are, I can make some sort of living. Only..." He stopped talking and faced me mournfully.

"Only I can neither weld nor ski."

I nodded sympathetically. My options for some sort of suitable response to Harper's problems were getting more and more limited.

We had reversed directions and were headed back to the street toward my house. I wedged my body next to his right arm in a reasoned effort to be so close to him he couldn't raise his clenched fist and damage me. I must have read about this defensive posture in a work of fiction.

Bowing slightly as we passed my house, he waved me toward my front door and then wordlessly continued down the street.

My wife had to know. Slumped disconsolately in an easy chair, I told her what had happened up to now. She remained calm. Before she could say anything, the phone rang. My wife answered and handed it to me. It was Chief Keresey.

"That was your nut case, eh, Mr. Caplin?"

"That was Bennett Harper," I advised the Chief. "And thanks for the escort."

He chuckled. "You recognized Detective Crowley in that unmarked sedan. It was his own private car, you know."

Thanking the Chief again for his solicitude, I managed to stammer out a request that had been simmering in my troubled mind ever since Harper had invaded my life.

"Chief, what does it take to get a gun permit?"

"I was wondering when you'd get around to that," Chief Keresey replied. "Mr. Caplin, if you don't mind my saying so, I don't think you're going to need that kind of weapon." The best I could hope for, the Chief advised me, was a permit to have the gun in my home. He could not promise me I'd get permission to carry a concealed weapon.

"Fact of the matter is, Mr. Caplin, that the pieces aren't much use in a case like the one we got here. Better you just watch your step and keep in constant touch with us."

In truth, I was relieved. Guns in a home with small children presented a hazard. Instead, I bought three baseball bats and placed them strategically around the house.

Two days after my last encounter with Harper, he resurfaced, at my office. My secretary, who knew all about his existence, confronted me on Tuesday morning with the news that "Mr. Bennett Harper wants to see you. Says it's very important."

"He knows I'm here?"

Rosalind paled. "I'm sorry. I never thought to tell him you were out of the office.

"Well, it won't make that much difference. He probably would've squatted in the waiting room until I came back." No reason for both my secretary and myself suffering. My own growing trepidation with each passing day that saw Bennett Harper loose and threatening was stress enough for one office force.

Harper looked quite normal as he entered my room. He sat down, unbidden, and faced me with that now familiar bland yet menacing lack of expression.

"I just found out something in the 'Mickey Mouse' daily comic strip," he announced.

"Oh," I responded with little enthusiasm. "What was that?"

Sounding as though he were ordering breakfast at a lunch counter, Bennett Harper responded, "It's all right to kill somebody if you say 'excuse me' first."

It was then I regretted taking Chief Keresey's advice in not applying for gun permit. Because if I had a pistol conveniently close, I do believe I'd have taken a shot at Harper.

It was mostly the cold assurance of his statement that appalled me. He meant it. He was informing me that his next move would be life-terminating, and the intended victim could be me, Al Capp, or—this might explain the extremity of my reaction—my wife and children.

That was all my visitor had to say. He remained embedded in his chair, studying me with that maddening composure which camouflaged his deadly (I was convinced) nature.

My secretary entered. "Your next appointment is waiting."

It didn't matter that there was no appointment; Rosalind knew my needs. At that moment I needed Bennett Harper out of my life.

Leaving as little as possible to chance, I researched my tormentor. His employers at Ethyl gasoline were guarded, but convinced I intended no mischief; they cooperated.

"Harper is, or was," I was told by his department head," a very able chemical engineer. A year or so ago he developed an infection in his foot.

It got to be quite serious. We sent him down to Johns Hopkins. Well, they treated him. Cured the infection. But..." Now my informant hesitated.

"How much of this do you want to know?"

I told him what had happened up to now. In detail. He sighed.

"O.K., you've got a handle on his problem. May as well tell you everything.

Everything involved Harper's attending physician at Johns Hopkins. This medical man, a surgeon, found his patient acting oddly. The surgeon brought in a psychiatrist who tested Harper and informed the Ethyl people that their chemical engineer had a serious mental problem.

What happened next was an effort by Ethyl to treat its employee. They secured the services of a psychiatrist and convinced Harper to begin treatment. Harper went to the doctor on a regular basis.

I phoned the psychiatrist. He listened and when he found out Harper's employers had given me his name, he relaxed his occupational vigilance and asked me how he could help me.

"Is he dangerous, Doctor?"

The doctor didn't hesitate, although his voice lost some of its professional calm. "After coming here on a regular basis, he suddenly began breaking his appointments. Never explained why. Never phoned for a postponement. The man just stopped coming." The psychiatrist sighed. "Although this was not an isolated experience, Bennett's attitude puzzled me. And then," he sighed again, and this time I detected a quiver in his exhalation. "Then, one day, leaving the office at about seven or so, I saw him. Yes, it was Harper." The doctor had stopped. I jangled the phone. Had I lost the connection?

No. The connection was still there. After several moments of silence, the psychiatrist continued. It was clear he was exerting real effort to control his voice.

"It was Harper, all right, hiding behind a bush on my front lawn. Staring. Just staring out from behind that bush. And even though it was beginning to get dark, there was no misreading his expression."

"That must have scared the hell out of you." I suspected that doctors have feelings too, and nerves!

"It did," he admitted.

"And you tell me he's dangerous?"

"In my judgment, very dangerous, Mr. Caplin."

A course for action seemed clear to me. "Why don't you have him committed, doctor? Letting a man like that roam around loose could lead to disaster."

At this, the psychiatrist lost his composure. His voice rose. "For Christ's sake, I don't want to see my brains splattered all over the front lawn."

"But doctor, I thought if they committed Harper, he'd be...well, you know, put away. Isn't that the way it works?"

"Sure, sure." The doctor laughed bitterly. "They put Harper away for how long—six months? A year? Then they examine him and before you can say Sigmund Freud, he's on the prowl again. And you know who—whom— he's going to prowl after? Me, the black-hearted villain who committed him. No, Mr. Caplin, I'm not setting myself up as a target for a dangerous schizoid like Bennett Harper."

This was a shattering experience for me. It began to look like I could count on no one to assist me in getting this would-be assassin out of my and my family's life.

Instead of enjoying Harper's extended period of silence, each succeeding day without some word or contact with him became more and more enervating. My work suffered and sleepless nights contributed nothing to my peace of mind.

Alfred phoned me from Cambridge.

"Who the hell is Bennett Harper?" he queried.

Even my plan to keep my brother out of this nightmare had failed. It was my impression that Harper had substituted me for Al Capp, and had forgotten that it was my brother, not I, who had created "Li'l Abner." Obviously, that subterfuge hadn't worked.

I told Alfred as much as I dared, skipping the psychiatrist's analysis of Harper's homicidal character.

"I suspected something like that when he phoned me at the studio," Alfred reported. "So I told him to call Charley Post."

Charles Post was Al Capp's lawyer. He was a tall mournful looking Midwesterner who, after graduating from Harvard, became more of a proper Bostonian than any existing member of the Cabots or the Lodges.

"What happened? Did Harper call Post?" I inquired.

"He did. They met in Charley's office with an Inspector from the Boston Police department acting like a lawyer. Charley says Harper is clearly not with it. He told them that he was reduced to wearing smoked glasses—"

"Because welders and ski instructors wear smoked glasses and those are the only professions open to him?"

"Right," Alfred agreed. "What comes next?"

I didn't know. But I reassured my brother that Bennett Harper would bother him no more. Alfred was content with my pledge of security. I was not.

Bennett Harper could not be arrested, no matter how dangerous he was. It was now that I learned about the agony of frustration that threatened people undergo because the law has no provisions for punishment for a "crime that hasn't been committed." No matter that all involved in this adventure agreed that an act of violence was expected. Until the "perpetrator perpetrated" all the shivering victim-to-be could do—was shiver!

The tensions became unbearable. The dreadful calm with which Harper had assured me that "it's all right to kill if you say 'excuse me' first," only added to my dread of the next confrontation with a man I was now convinced regarded me as his mortal enemy.

Brooding about all this in my den on a cheerless Sunday, deliberately isolated from my wife and children, I reviewed my options and wound up with the harrowing conclusion that I had none. From behind my closed door, I heard my wife's voice.

"Phone call for you, dear. It's Chief Keresey."

What now? I walked into the bedroom and picked up the phone. Chief Keresey sounded jubilant. "We got the son of a bitch!"

The son of a bitch could only be... "You mean Bennett Harper?"

"Nobody else," the chief exulted. "The Feds nabbed the loony."

"The feds? But how—I mean...you say the Feds? Members of the Federal government?"

The chief chuckled. "Wait 'til you hear this. The nut actually got into Snyder's office."

"Snyder—the Secretary of the Treasury? That Snyder?"

"Nobody else but." Chief Keresey was bubbling.

Here's how Bennett Harper managed to get into the private office of a member of President Truman's cabinet. He had phoned for an appointment giving as a credential his position with the Ethyl Gasoline people and hinting that it was a matter of grave national import that prompted his request for an audience with the Secretary of the Treasury.

The appointment was made and Harper showed up at the Treasury Department promptly at 11 a.m.

Admitted to Secretary Snyder's office, Harper pulled out of his pocket a copy of the Washington Post and held up the comic page for the puzzled Secretary to study. He pointed to the comic strip, "Abbie and Slats," illustrated by Raeburn Van Buren and written by—me.

This comic strip had been created by Al Capp, who had convinced the superb Saturday Evening Post illustrator, Rae Van Buren, that his future would be assured with a successful strip. Rae agreed, and "Abbie and Slats" became an instant success.

After seven years of writing and drawing "Abner" and writing "Abbie and Slats," Alfred tired of the demanding routine and asked me (by phone from London) would I please write a week or so of the feature and thus satisfy the deadline-conscious Van Buren clamoring for more copy.

The "week or so" requested by Alfred was now in its tenth year. I wrote it and enjoyed doing so. The characters were raffish and unwashed, the most raffish and unwashed of those being "Bathless Groggins." In the farcical continuity waved in Secretary Snyder's face Bathless had managed to isolate Ft. Knox, repository of our nation's gold reserve, and—at least for the moment—was the sole possessor of a vast quantity of precious ingots.

"That money," Bennett Harper informed the puzzled Secretary, "belongs to me."

Mr. Snyder must have decided to hear Harper out. He listened as Bennett Harper explained with careful attention to detail that he owned Fort Knox and that if the money now accrued by Bathless Groggins was not returned immediately to its rightful owner, Harper, "you, Mr. Secretary, will have to suffer the consequences."

It was then that Secretary Snyder summoned help and Bennett Harper was forcibly escorted from the Treasury building to a waiting ambulance. He was charged with threatening the life of a federal officer and put behind bars.

My relief was audible. My wife rushed into my den when she heard the banshee yowling of a man whose death sentence had just been commuted.

"The crazy bastard is in the slammer," I howled, bounding up and down in an ecstasy of relief.

"Bennett Harper?"

"The same," I exulted. "Seems he threatened the life and limb of Secretary of the Treasury Snyder, and that's a federal no no."

"What will they do to him?" my wife asked.

"Well, Chief Keresey said when they—the Washington people—realized that Harper was a mental case the head doctors took over. He's now in some hospital and the Chief says he'll be a ward of the Federal government for a long, long time!"

This all happened over 20 years ago.

But I often find myself looking fixedly at men who are about 6 feet 2 in height, weigh over 200 pounds, have a straight rather abbreviated nose, sandy hair, wear thick-lensed glasses, and have pock marked skin.

After all, I've said time and time again, maybe Bennett Harper was cured and no longer had to wear smoked glasses to make a living.

But suppose he had a relapse?

To this day I study with nervous intensity approaching strangers who are about 6 feet 2...etc...etc.

Post Script

This was written by the 12-and-a-half-year-old Alfred Caplin three years after he lost his leg in an accident when a trolley car ran over him. It is the only recorded reaction of Al Capp to an event that altered his life and the lives of those close to him.

I

When I endeavor to look back onto the past, a vision, a dim vision obstructed by dark clouds, comes back to me.

I am in a garden, a beautiful garden where there are sweet-smelling roses and grape arbors with their luscious fruit hanging temptingly. There are apple trees in the garden, apple trees overladen with myriads of red fruit, and the grass is green. There is Happiness in that garden.

For ten happy years I dwelt in this garden, unconscious of the evils outside its gates, kept busy with study and recreation. I had companions in this garden, other children, red-cheeked children, crowing, joyful children.

But one day, one sad day, I ventured out of this garden, hand in hand with the false siren Curiosity. I walked, amazed at the clanging noisy world—not at all like the peaceful garden that I had left behind me—forever.

There came a great noise—a great cry—a crash—and darkness.

And the gate of the garden closed.

II

Months passed—a year came and was gone in what seemed to me an age. It was an age of whiteness. A white bed, white-clad nurses, white-clad doctors, shining white instruments—White—a horribly ghastly age of Whiteness.

III

When the year passed, I arose from my sick-bed and hastened to the garden. I saw there the same companions of my childhood playing in it. I hammered at its gate. The children ran to the fence and spoke a few words of pity to me and then resumed their frolics. And to this day, I sit at the

147

gate, vainly waiting for the day when I may enter. Sometimes the children come to the edge of the gate and speak a few words of pity to me—but not for long. They hear the call of health and, hastening back, resume their play.